W9-DHN-721

DISCARDED
7-12-2022

Digital Cameras
and Camcorders

OTHER TITLES IN THE TECHNOLOGY 360 SERIES:

Cell Phones

E-books

Electric Cars

Global Positioning Systems

iPod® and MP3 Players

Online Schools

Online Social Networking

Robots

Rollercoasters

Video Games

Web 2.0

Digital Cameras and Camcorders

BY STUART A. KALLEN

LUCENT BOOKS
A part of Gale, Cengage Learning

GALE
CENGAGE Learning·

Farmington Hills, Mich • San Francisco • New York • Waterville, Maine
Meriden, Conn • Mason, Ohio • Chicago

GALE
CENGAGE Learning®

©2014 Gale, Cengage Learning

WCN: 01-100-101

LIBRARY OF CONGRESS CATALOGING-IN-PUBLICATION DATA

Kallen, Stuart A., 1955-
  Digital cameras and camcorders / Stuart A. Kallen.
    pages cm. -- (Technology 360)
  Includes bibliographical references and index.
  ISBN 978-1-4205-0165-0 (hardcover)
 1. Digital cameras--Juvenile literature. 2. Photography--Digital techniques--Juvenile literature. 3. Camcorders--Juvenile literature. I. Title.
  TR256.K35 2014
  771.3--dc23
                              2013045910

Lucent Books
27500 Drake Rd
Farmington Hills MI 48331

ISBN-13: 978-1-4205-0165-0
ISBN-10: 1-4205-0165-8

Printed in the United States of America
1 2 3 4 5 6 7 18 17 16 15 14

CONTENTS

"As we go forward, I hope we're going to continue to use technology to make really big differences in how people live and work."
—Sergey Brin, co-founder of Google

The past few decades have seen some amazing advances in technology. Many of these changes have had a direct and measureable impact on the way people live, work, and play. Communication tools such as cell phones, satellites, and the Internet allow people to keep in constant contact across longer distances and from the most remote places. In fields related to medicine, existing technologies—digital imaging devices, robotics, and lasers, for example—are being used to redefine surgical procedures and diagnostic techniques. As technology has become more complex, however, so have the related ethical, legal, and safety issues.

Psychologist B.F. Skinner once noted that "the real problem is not whether machines think but whether men do." Recent advances in technology have, in many cases, drastically changed the way people view the world around them. They can have a conversation with someone across the globe at lightening speed, access a huge universe of information with the click of a key, or become an avatar in a virtual world of their own making. While such advances have been viewed as a great boon in some quarters, they have also opened the door to questions about whether or not the speed of technological advancement has come at an unspoken price. A closer examination of the evolution and use of these devices provides a deeper understanding of the social, cultural, and ethical implications that they may hold for our future.

Technology 360 not only explores how evolving technologies work, but also examines the short- and long-term impact of their use on society as a whole. Each volume in Technology 360 focuses on a particular invention, device, or family of similar devices, and explores how the device was developed, how it works, its impact on society, and possible future uses. Volumes also contain a timeline specific to each topic, a glossary of technical terms used in the text, and a subject index. Sidebars, photos, detailed illustrations, tables, charts, and graphs help further illuminate the text.

Titles in this series emphasize inventions and devices familiar to most readers, such as robotics, digital cameras, iPods, and video games. Not only will users get an easy-to-understand, "nuts and bolts" overview of these inventions, they will also learn just how much these devices have evolved. For example, in 1973 a Motorola cell phone weighed about 2 pounds (.907kg) and cost $4,000—today, cell phones weigh only a few ounces and are inexpensive enough for every member of the family to have one. Lasers—long a staple of the industrial world—have become highly effective surgical tools, capable of reshaping the cornea of the eye and cleaning clogged arteries. Early video games were played on large machines in arcades; now, many families play games on sophisticated home systems that allow for multiple players and cross-location networking.

IMPORTANT DATES IN THE DEVELOPMENT

1913–1914
35mm film and cameras are developed.

1962
Ampex introduces the VR-1500 video tape recorder as the first video recording system for home use. The camera weighs about 100 pounds.

1827
French inventor Joseph Nicéphore Niépce creates the first photographic image using a *camera obscura*.

1948
The first Polaroid cameras, which use a one-step photographic system developed by Edwin H. Land, are introduced.

1889
Thomas Edison commissions William Kennedy Laurie Dickson to create the first motion-picture camera, the Kinetograph.

| 1850 | 1875 | 1900 | 1925 | 1950 | 1960 |

1885
The Eastman Company introduces the first transparent photographic film.

1951
The first video tape recorder is used to capture live images from television cameras and save the information on magnetic videotapes.

1900
Eastman Kodak introduces the Brownie, the first mass-market camera.

1923
The home movie era begins with the introduction of Kodak's 16mm film, cameras, and projectors.

OF DIGITAL CAMERAS AND CAMCORDERS

1985
Lucasfilm develops the Pixar Image Computer, a machine with large computing capacity and the ability to capture very high-resolution images.

1997
Philippe Kahn, a camera phone technology pioneer, becomes the first person to wirelessly transmit photos using a cell phone.

1983
Sony and JVC introduce the first consumer camcorders in competing tape formats, Betamax and VHS.

2005
YouTube begins operations.

1975   1980   1985   1995   2000   2005

1977
The first point-and-shoot autofocus camera, the Konica C35 AF, is introduced.

1989
The first commercially-available digital camera, the Fuji DS-X, is sold in Japan. Other digital cameras are sold in the United States a year later.

2000
The first commercially available mobile phones with built-in cameras are sold in Japan and South Korea.

1984
The first digital still cameras are used by Canon to capture and transmit photographs during the Summer Olympic Games.

A New View on the World

People love to snap photos of their families, places they have visited, and even their pets. This being the case, the art of photography continues to grow even though the way pictures are taken has changed. Until the end of the 1990s, most pictures were shot with photographic film with names such as Kodachrome and Fujicolor. Most film consisted of long rolls of thin plastic capable of holding twelve, twenty-four, or thirty-six photos.

Photographic film was coated with light-sensitive silver halide salts. When a photographer clicked a picture, light entered the camera and impressed images on the chemicals on the film. In order to see the pictures after they were taken, film had to be developed. Developing photos entailed treating the film with other chemicals, which created negative images. Negatives were used to print pictures on photographic paper, which involved another chemical process. Most photographers had their film developed and printed at drugstores and other retailers that specialized in photo processing. Undeveloped rolls also could be mailed to large centralized plants that processed thousands of rolls a day.

Photography with film was expensive and time-consuming. Purchasing, developing, and printing a thirty-six-picture roll of film could cost $10 to $15 in the early 1990s. Oftentimes only a few pictures on a roll would be memorable or worth saving. In addition, if only two or three pictures were taken at an event, film might sit in the camera for weeks, months, or even years before the roll was completely used and taken in for printing. Despite the hassles, about 60 billion film photos were shot worldwide in 1995, at the height of the film era.

The Digital Era

When the first digital cameras went on sale in 1999, the decades-old tradition of shooting, developing, and printing film moved toward extinction. Digital cameras are miniature computers that completely changed the photographic process. They replaced expensive film and chemicals with microchips that instantly created photos using battery-powered electricity. The idea was extremely popular, and interest in digital photography continued to grow after the first cell phone cameras were introduced in 2002. By the following year, more camera phones were sold worldwide than stand-alone digital cameras. By 2006, half of the world's mobile phones had built-in cameras.

As digital camera sales soared, so, too, did the number of photographs taken. Because digital photos were so easy to upload to computers, and e-mail, and to post to websites,

Popular photography began shortly after the introduction of the Kodak camera in 1888 (back left). The evolving designs of Kodak cameras include folding cameras, box brownies, instamatics, and a 1999 digital camera (front center).

there was a growing demand for photo-sharing and social media sites such as Facebook, which was founded in 2004. By 2013, around 300 million digital photos were being uploaded to Facebook every day, and this was only one among dozens of popular photo-sharing websites, which included Picasa, Instagram, and Flickr.

Video Sharing

Digital cameras can also capture moving images, and shooting and sharing homemade videos was another part of the social media boom during the 2000s. The video-sharing website YouTube was launched in 2005; within six months, people were uploading more than sixty-five thousand new videos a day and the site was attracting more than 100 million daily viewers. By 2013, forty-eight hours of video were being uploaded to YouTube every minute, which resulted in nearly eight years' worth of content posted every single day.

Digital video cameras provided new ways for people to report on cultural and current events. Videos covering everything from religious festivals in India to environmental problems in Africa can be seen on YouTube. Citizen reporters can post videos of demonstrations, disasters, and war.

Even as digital cameras were responsible for spreading truth and inviting change, there was a downside to the photo- and video-sharing trend. Camera phones have peeled away a layer of privacy people used to take for granted. Countless unapproved images have been taken in locker rooms, at bars, and at parties and posted on social media websites without the subjects' permission. In addition, camera phones have been used by students to cheat on tests, by spies to steal company secrets, and in courtrooms to expose the identities of undercover police officers.

Whatever the drawbacks, digital cameras have become an integral part of modern society. According to Samsung, more than 2.5 billion people around the globe owned digital cameras in 2013. These devices have transformed the way people see themselves and document the world in ways that were unimaginable even twenty years ago.

CHAPTER 1

Dissecting a Digital Camera

The word photography is composed of two Greek words, *photon* (light) and *graphos* (drawing). Digital cameras transform light into photographic imagery.

In technical terms, light is electromagnetic radiation visible to the human eye. Light is sometimes described as light waves, photons, or particles of light. When a digital camera takes a photograph, particles of light enter the lens, which focuses the light on a silicon microchip called an image sensor. The light is converted into electrical digital information represented by bits and bytes, the language of computers. Another microchip assembles the bits and bytes into a photographic file. This file can be displayed on a monitor, e-mailed, uploaded to a website, or sent to a printer. While digital cameras are used to take millions of photographs every day, they are complex and remarkable devices.

Powering Up

Digital cameras come in all shapes and sizes, from tiny keychain cameras to $2,500 digital single lens reflexes (DSLRs). Stand-alone digital cameras, sometimes called point-and-shoot, are those that are not part of cell phones, tablet computers, or music players. These cameras contain their working parts in a case made from metal and plastic.

A Samsung digital camera with smartphone and zoom lens is tested at a 2012 tradeshow.

Every digital camera relies on batteries to power electronic parts. These are contained in a battery compartment, which is accessible through a latched door on the camera body. The electric power is transferred to various camera components through chrome-plated steel strips that come in contact with the battery. Power is activated by a power switch or button, most often located on or near the top of the camera body.

Lens: The Eye of the Camera

When a camera is powered up and pointed at a subject, the lens acts as the "eye." Like a human eye, the lens absorbs visible light waves reflecting off objects. Like the lens of an eye, the camera lens is slightly curved, or convex. The convex shape refracts, or bends, incoming light waves so that they converge at a single point called the focal point, which is on the image sensor. If a person could look inside a camera pointed at a candle, for example, they would see a tiny image of that candle at the focal point.

Without lenses it would be impossible to create high-quality photographs, prompting renowned landscape photographer Ansel Adams to comment, "There is something magical about the image formed by the lens. Surely every serious photographer stands in some awe of this miraculous device."[1]

A Variety of Lens Lengths

Another fascinating feature of the lens concerns its ability to make distant objects appear closer or close objects appear distant. This power is determined by what is called the focal length of the lens. Focal length is measured in millimeters (mm).

Telephoto lenses, which magnify distant objects, are typically 135mm or longer. These lenses are useful for wild animal photography, sports events, or any place where the

The Wide-Angle Lens

Photographer Melissa Martin Ellis explains the pros and cons of wide-angle lenses:

Wide-angle lenses are definitely the lens of choice in cramped conditions, such as small rooms or other situations where you can't back up far enough to include everything you want in the picture if you use a normal lens. Their wider field of view makes them great for scenic outdoor photography as well, especially if your subject is a sweeping panorama and you want to get as much of it as you can in your shot. . . .

It is easy to get distorted images with wide-angle lenses, which makes them inappropriate for taking closeups of people. Wide-angle lenses used for closeups will distort the faces of your subjects. They make the features closest to the lens (like noses) bigger and those farther away from the lens (ears, for instance) smaller. Because they capture more of a scene, people and objects at the edges of wide-angle shots can also appear distorted.

Melissa Martin Ellis. "Types of Lenses." *NetPlaces: Photography*, 2013. www.netplaces.com/photography/the-world-through-a-lens/types-of-lenses.htm.

action is far from the photographer. However, photographs taken with a telephoto lens often have a flat appearance and background objects appear blurry.

Wide-angle lenses are much shorter than telephotos, around 28mm. Because these types of lenses are extremely curved, wide-angles allow more of a scene, or a wider area, to be photographed. Wide-angle lenses are useful for landscape photography or taking pictures of buildings. An ultra-wide-angle lens, with a 15mm focal length, is called a fish-eye. This type of lens provides a round, distorted view of 180 degrees.

The most versatile type of lens is called a zoom. These lenses move back and forth, guided by a tiny electronic motor that is operated by a switch on the camera body. The movement changes the focal length. A zoom rated 28-70mm can be set anywhere between a wide-angle and a slight telephoto. In addition to focal length, zooms are rated by how many times they magnify a distant object when the lens is fully extended. A 10x zoom makes objects appear ten times closer, while a 30x zoom brings objects thirty times closer.

Attachable lenses for a professional DSLR camera come in a variety of lengths, including telephoto and zoom.

The magnifying power of the human eye falls somewhere between wide-angle and telephoto lenses. A 50mm lens matches human vision. Most cell phones and inexpensive stand-alone cameras are equipped with 50mm lenses. Photographers who use DSLRs can swap lenses on the camera depending on the shooting conditions and needs of the photographer.

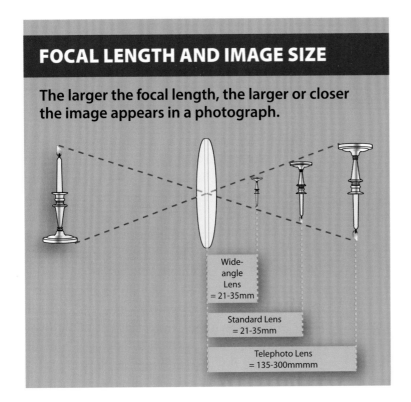

FOCAL LENGTH AND IMAGE SIZE

The larger the focal length, the larger or closer the image appears in a photograph.

Wide-angle Lens = 21-35mm

Standard Lens = 21-35mm

Telephoto Lens = 135-300mmmm

Lens Elements

While a lens can be one single piece of convex glass, most camera lenses are extremely elaborate devices. Zoom lenses have more than one hundred parts, including numerous pieces of glass linked to motors, springs, rings, and rotating linkages called cams. All are assembled together in a lens body called a barrel.

Individual glass lenses joined together perform the main work of a lens, which is processing light. Each piece of lens glass is called an element. Elements are covered with special mineral coatings that maintain proper light transmission and color balance, and prevent reflection. When two or more elements are joined together it is called an optical group. Inexpensive cameras might have one or two optical groups. A basic zoom lens has at least three specific moving optical groups, plus one stationary optical group. The four optical groups, front to back, are the focus group, the variator group, the compensator group, and the master group.

As the name suggests, the focus group moves back and forth to bring objects into focus. The photographer can either rotate an outer ring called the focus collar by hand or press a button to activate the power focus function. The power focus function activates a device called a ring ultrasonic motor. This circular electronic motor is responsible for moving the focus group.

The variator group is responsible for the zoom feature. It varies the magnification power of the lens by changing the focal length. The variator group is also operated by a ring ultrasonic motor.

The job of the compensator group is to maintain proper focus when the lens zooms in and out. Without this group, the subject would go out of focus when the variator moves.

The last group, called the non-moving master group, relays the various magnifications from the other groups to the image sensor.

Some zoom lenses have extra elements, groups, and motors that can add quite a bit of weight to the lens. For example, the Nikon 28-70mm zoom has fifteen elements in eleven groups. It weighs more than 2 pounds (.9k)—as much as the Nikon DSLR to which it is attached. This lens alone is nearly seven times as heavy as an entire iPhone.

Photographers are willing to carry the extra weight because the heavy lenses provide better photos. As technology blogger Marc Spiwak explains, "If the lens itself generates a lousy image, there's no way the rest of the camera can compensate for that deficiency. . . . Lenses take up space and that's all there is to it."[2]

The Aperture: Light Control

Another piece of the lens is called the aperture, which means opening. This mechanical device is located either directly in front of, or inside, the master group. The aperture controls the amount of light that enters the camera. With too little

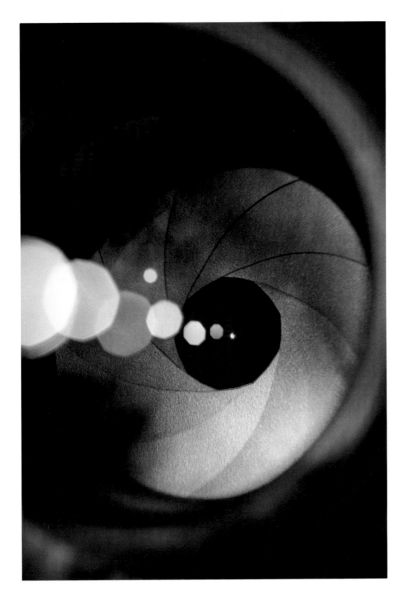

A close-up view through a lens shows the rings of the camera aperture, which controls the amount of light allowed to enter.

light a photo is dark, or underexposed. With too much light it is overexposed. In most stand-alone cameras, the aperture is made from a group of overlapping plates called the iris diaphragm. These plates move to provide a larger or smaller opening, letting in more or less light.

The size of the aperture is designated by a number called an f-stop. The larger the f-stop number, the smaller the aperture. For example, f/8 indicates that the aperture is "stopped down" to let in less light. An f/1.4 setting would open the aperture very wide to take photos in low-light settings. Average lenses have six to eight f-stops, including f/2.8, f/4, and f/5.6. Most cell phones and inexpensive digital cameras have set apertures that cannot be changed. They are usually fixed at f/2.8 or f/4.

Shutter: The Curtain

The camera shutter is not part of the lens, but is located in the camera body between the lens and the image sensor. The shutter is like a curtain; it snaps open for a millisecond to let light flood onto the image sensor, and then quickly snaps shut. The shutter is operated by the shutter release button, the main control on top of a camera.

The amount of time a shutter stays open is called shutter speed. This speed is designated by fractions of a second, such as 1/30th of a second or 1/250th of a second. The higher the shutter speed, the faster the shutter opens and closes. With longer shutter speeds, more light is let into the camera.

A shutter must obtain highly reliable, accurate speeds, which makes it another intricate mechanical part of the camera. The opening and closing action is determined by a series of gears, springs, and switches that are activated when the shutter release button is pushed.

Cell phone cameras and inexpensive point-and-shoot models do not have precise mechanical shutters. They have what is called an electronic shutter. This is a somewhat misleading name because there is no shutter at all. When a picture is taken on a cell phone, the image sensor rapidly switches on and off. The average shutter speed on an image sensor is 1/60th of a second. Some cameras can achieve electronic shutter speeds as high as 1/1000th of a second.

Framing a View with a Viewfinder

Setting up, or framing, a photograph involves viewing a subject and moving the camera to get the best shot. With most stand-alone digital cameras, this can be done with a viewfinder located above the lens. The photographer peers through the viewfinder and gets an idea of what the final shot will look like. In point-and-shoot models, viewfinders are independent of the lens; they do not necessarily present the exact view that will appear in the photo. For example, objects at the edges of the frame might not appear in the final shot.

Digital single lens reflex cameras have what is called through-the-lens (TTL) viewing. With a TTL system, the photographer views exactly what the lens sees. The system works through a series of movable mirrors located at the back of the lens, which reflect images to the viewfinder or liquid crystal display (LCD), where the photographer can see it.

While not all digital cameras have viewfinders, they all feature an electronic flat-panel monitor called an LCD. These thin, lightweight panels are found on nearly every digital product, including cameras, watches, music players, and television sets. While LCDs are commonplace, they are extremely complicated instruments.

A man reviews an image on the LCD viewfinder of a Canon 7D digital camera at a safari park.

An LCD is made of two pieces of glass that contain a liquid crystal material between them. When electricity is supplied, the molecules of the liquid crystal align to allow varying levels of light to pass through them. In a camera, this works to create images on the LCD that have been transmitted from the lens.

While the science behind LCDs is extremely technical, the screens make framing a photo simple. However, in bright light, an LCD can be very difficult to view. Some photographers address this problem by adding an inexpensive LCD hood to their camera. The hood is a three- or four-sided awning that fits over the LCD to shade it from bright light. Some digital cameras feature LCDs that tilt and twist. This allows the photographer to view the screen from different angles when the light produces glare. Twisting or tilting LCDs also let photographers shoot with the camera above the head, low to the ground, or even take pictures around corners.

The Image Sensor

While LCDs, lenses, and shutters perform important roles, the image sensor is the heart of a digital camera. Most image sensors are 35mm wide and 24mm high (1.3 by .94 inches), about the same size as the 35mm film commonly used during the pre-digital era. Image sensors come in two styles, a charge-coupled device (CCD) and a complementary metal-oxide semiconductor (CMOS). Both types produce photographs in a similar manner, as photography expert David D. Busch explains:

> [There] is little need to understand the technical difference between them, or even which type of sensor resides in your camera. Early in the game, CCDs were the imager of choice for high-quality image capture, while CMOS chips were the "cheapie" alternative used for less critical applications. Today, technology has advanced so that CMOS sensors have overcome virtually all the advantages CCD sensors formerly had, so that CMOS has become the dominant image capture device, with only a few cameras using CCDs remaining.[3]

Pixels into Pictures

Whether an image sensor is a CCD or a CMOS, it has a light-sensitive area called a photodiode. The photodiode is filled with millions of microscopic cavities called photosites, which are set in a grid pattern. When the shutter of a digital camera snaps open, photosites absorb photons of light and convert them into electrons—particles with an electrical charge. This conversion process, called the photoelectric effect, is similar to the way solar cells convert sunlight to electricity.

After light undergoes the photoelectric effect on the image sensor, it is transferred to a microchip called an analog-to-digital converter (ADC). The ADC converts the light into electronic dots called pixels. Each pixel contains specific digital information that defines its color and brightness. A digital photograph consists of millions of pixels; individual pixels are too small to see without magnification. The eye naturally blends pixels together to create what appears to be a solid image.

The pixels from the ADC are sent to a computer chip called a digital image processor. This device contains software that reconstructs a full-color image from the output of the image sensor. This process is called demosaicing. In

A magnified view of an image shows the pixels—the squares of information that make up a digital image.

The Invention of the Digital Camera

In 1975 Eastman Kodak engineer Steven Sasson developed the first digital camera. It weighed 8 pounds (3.6k) and was about the size of microwave oven. It took twenty-three seconds to shoot a single black-and-white photograph. Each picture was ten thousand pixels—1 percent of a megapixel. After another twenty-three seconds, the picture could be viewed on a television screen attached to the camera. With this invention, the age of digital photography was born.

It would be sixteen more years before Kodak made the first commercially available digital camera. The DCS-100 took pictures with a charge-coupled device (CCD) image sensor encased in a Nikon camera body. The device was attached to a huge 55-pound (25k) external pack containing electronics, batteries, and a 200-megabyte hard drive capable of holding only 156 images. In 1991 the DCS-100 sold for $13,000 and had a resolution of 1.3 megapixels. Since that time, image sensors have improved dramatically, even as their prices fell. For example, in 2013, a keychain camera with a 5-megapixel image sensor could be found for as little as $10.

the simplest terms, the digital image processor arranges the pixels so they appear as a photograph.

Because of the importance of pixels, a camera is rated by the number its image processor can produce. A megapixel is one million pixels, and cameras with a higher number of megapixels take photos with higher resolution. Higher resolution means more details can be seen. In 2013 most smartphones had 5- to 8-megapixel cameras. A high-quality 16-megapixel camera can be purchased for under $100, while a top-of-the-line DSLR with 36.3 megapixels costs around $2,800.

Storing Photos

Once light becomes pixels, it is a photograph represented in digital language. This digital data is permanently stored on the camera's flash memory card. Before it gets to the memory card, it passes through a microchip called a memory buffer. The buffer is important, because it determines the speed of the digital data as it moves from the image sensor to the memory. If a camera's buffer is slow, it can freeze the camera for a few seconds as the file passes to the flash memory. This could cause a photographer to miss important shots.

The majority of flash memory cards in digital cameras are in the secure digital (SD) format. SD cards are small, relatively inexpensive, and designed to hold large amounts of data. For example, a 32-gigabyte (GB) SD card can store more than fourteen thousand high-quality pictures from a 10-megapixel camera. The memory card is located in a slot with a small door. Photographers can switch memory cards when they are full, or remove them to download pictures onto a computer using a memory card reader.

The Flash

Because it takes a lot of light to expose a photo, the flash is one of the most important features of a camera. The flash produces very bright light for a very short time, usually between 1/200th and 1/1000th of a second. The flash is linked to the camera's shutter. When the shutter release button is pressed, it triggers the flash.

Most, but not all, digital cameras have built-in flashes located above the lens in the camera body. While built-in flashes meet the needs of most photographers, some use portable flash units. These are removable devices that attach to a camera body on a mount called a hot shoe. While a built-in flash can illuminate subjects up to 10 feet (3m) away, a portable flash extends that range to 30 feet (9m).

Whatever the style of flash, it has three major parts: a gas discharge tube, a power supply, and a circuit connecting the tube to the power. The gas discharge tube produces the flash and functions like a neon or florescent light. It is a glass tube filled with xenon gas. A metal trigger plate runs through the middle of the tube. When electricity is applied, the xenon gas atoms are energized, causing them to emit visible light. A reflector behind the bulb directs light toward the subject.

Functions and Features

The main circuit board of a digital camera houses several other items that aid the photographic process. A quartz timer is a little silver device that synchronizes all the functions of the various microprocessors so that they operate in harmony. Various circuits, called resistors and capacitors, act as fuses to protect electrical elements from power surges. Cameras also have one or more light-emitting diodes (LEDs) attached to the circuit board. These glow or flash when the power is on and when the camera is performing various functions.

Many digital cameras have speakers that emit a click or some other sound when the shutter release button is pressed. This sound is called auditory feedback and lets the photographer know that a picture has been snapped.

Most digital cameras can also record short movies. They record sound with small microphones that are built into the camera body. Cameras with a zoom function have thumb-operated buttons or dials that activate the mini motors that move the lens. Another important control on the camera is the function button. This allows the photographer to navigate through a camera's software menu, which is displayed on the LCD. By maneuvering the function button, photographers can perform many tasks. They can scroll through pictures stored in the camera, erase unwanted shots, and set manual controls that govern shutter speed, aperture, and other functions.

Built-in Wi-Fi is another popular function available on many digital cameras. Wi-Fi first appeared on Apple laptop computers in 1999. It works by broadcasting digital in-

Digital Single Lens Reflex Cameras

Digital cameras come in a variety of styles, including smartphones, ultra compacts, and point-and-shoot models. Digital single lens reflex (DSLR) cameras deliver the highest image quality. DSLRs feature interchangeable lenses, which provide the option of switching between a standard 55mm lens and a telephoto, wide-angle, macro, close-up, or other specialized lens. The lenses lock and unlock from a lens mount on the front of the camera.

Whatever type of lens is used, DSLRs feature through-the-lens (TTL) viewing, which allows photographers to see the exact image as it appears in front of the lens. TTL viewing works with four mirrors. The scene that passes through the lens strikes what is called a reflex mirror, which sits at a forty-five-degree angle inside the camera chamber. The light travels to a five-sided piece of glass, an optical element called a pentaprism. This bounces the light upward through two separate mirrors into the viewfinder. When the shutter release button is pushed, the reflex mirror springs out of the way as the shutter snaps.

The most expensive DSLRs have extremely high-resolution image sensors. For example, in 2012 Nikon came out with the D800, which features a 36.3-megapixel CMOS image sensor for shooting ultra-sharp photos. Sold without a lens, the camera body alone costs around $3,000.

formation wirelessly on radio waves using a small built-in device called a wireless network interface controller. Since the early 2000s, Wi-Fi has been incorporated into dozens of devices, including video games, smartphones, tablets, digital music players, and cameras. Wi-Fi lets users transfer photos wirelessly from their camera to a computer, website, or another Wi-Fi-equipped camera. In 2013 some of the most popular point-and-shoot cameras, such as the Nikon

COOLPIX and Canon PowerShot, offered Wi-Fi options. Most DSLR models also offered Wi-Fi.

Those with older cameras can take advantage of wireless convenience with Eye-Fi, an SD memory card with a Wi-Fi antenna built into the device. Users insert the Eye-Fi into their camera and, after pictures are taken, the device automatically uploads the photos to their computer.

Global Positioning System (GPS) technology is another digital camera option that relies on wireless transmission of data. Photographers use GPS in a process called geotagging, which pinpoints exactly where a photograph was taken. GPS works with space-based satellites that send signals to small receiver modules built into cameras. The data includes geographic coordinates such as latitude and longitude, which specify the camera's position at an exact point on the earth's surface. The data can also include altitude, time, and other information.

A High-tech Wonder

Digital cameras can be as small as a credit card or fit into a cell phone. But cameras pack a massive amount of power into a small package. With the ability to shoot crisp, clear pictures in all sorts of conditions and store thousands of photos, the modern camera is a high-tech wonder. It performs hundreds of functions at the press of a button and preserves single moments in time in photographs that can last forever.

CHAPTER 2

Camera Modes and Settings

A digital camera is a sophisticated computer. Like all computers, digital cameras rely on operating system (OS) software to function properly. The OS software is called firmware. This type of software is closely tied to specific hardware. In a digital camera, this hardware includes the lens, shutter, and LCD. Like other computers, digital cameras store firmware in a read-only memory (ROM), a built-in memory chip that is not usually modified or changed.

In addition to controlling a camera's hardware, firmware contains preprogrammed settings called modes. These are used for taking photographs in specific conditions, such as outdoors, at sports events, or at night. The photographer can select choices by turning a mode dial that features a menu represented by letters or icons. When the camera is in a specific mode, the firmware activates various devices, such as a light meter and an autofocus sensor, which analyze the scene. The camera then selects the appropriate settings for the lens, aperture, shutter, flash unit, and image sensor.

Smartphones also contain modes, but instead of turning a physical dial, they are accessed from the LCD screen. Unlike firmware in stand-alone cameras, camera operating systems in smartphones can be changed and augmented. Users can download a wide range of photography apps from the Internet. This software allows smartphone users to manipulate their photos in numerous ways.

Autofocus

Whether a camera is a smartphone, an ultra compact, or a DSLR, one of the initial functions of the firmware is to ensure a subject is in focus before a photograph is taken. This is done with two types of autofocus (AF) systems, active and passive. Most point-and-shoot cameras use active autofocus. This is controlled by a small round sensor located next to the lens. The AF sensor sends out pulses of invisible infrared light rays. The infrared beams bounce off a subject and reflect back to the camera at the speed of light. The camera's software computes the time between the outgoing infrared pulses and the incoming pulses, which allows it to judge distance. The software sends a signal to a mini motor on the focus group in the lens. The group moves backward or forward to bring the subject into focus. The process is continually active until the photographer presses the shutter release button.

Active AF works well in low light and at distances of up to 20 feet (6m). It also lets the camera track moving subjects that are far away from the photographer. Active AF does not work on subjects that are very close. Active AF is useless when shooting through windows, because the glass reflects the infrared beam. This prevents the camera from focusing on the scene beyond the window.

Many smartphones and DSLRs use a system called passive autofocus. Instead of relying on an infrared beam to actively judge distance, passive AF uses the camera's software to analyze the subject in the lens. The software evaluates the contrast in the image—the difference between the lightest and darkest parts of a scene. It also looks for blurriness or sharpness in different parts of an image. With this information, the software triggers a mini motor to adjust the lens to achieve the best focus.

Passive AF does not work well in low light or when pointed at a single-color surface, such as a white wall. Because active and passive AF have their own positive and negative qualities, many DSLRs offer both types of autofocus. This allows photographers to choose the best system for specific conditions.

Apertures and Depth of Field

Another aspect of a photo's focus is called depth of field (DOF). This term defines the zone of a photograph, from front to back, where the main subject is in sharp focus. There are two ways to describe depth of field: shallow or deep. Shallow depth of field is when the focus range is very narrow; the subjects in focus are between 2 inches to 2 feet (50mm to 600mm) from the camera. Deep depth of field is when the focus range is between about 6 feet (2m) and infinity.

This image of sunflowers was shot with a shallow depth of field by using a low f-stop setting, which resulted in a blurring out of the flowers in the background.

APERTURE AND DEPTH OF FIELD

The camera lens's aperture regulates the amount of light that can pass through it. The smaller the aperture, the larger the area that can be in focus in the photograph.

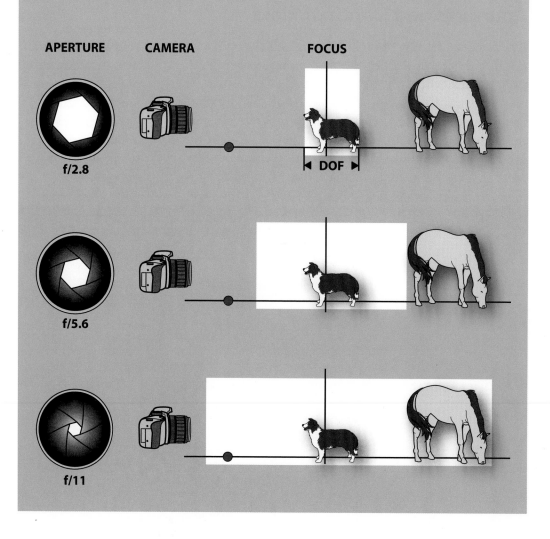

Depth of field is determined by the aperture setting. A low f-stop, such as f/1.4 or f/2.8, provides a shallow depth of field. This might be desirable if a photographer wanted to shoot a picture of a single rose on a bush while blurring out the leaves and branches behind the flower. A small f-stop number results in a large aperture opening.

A large f-stop number provides the deepest depth of field. If the photographer wanted to take a picture of an entire rose bush, along with a mountain range in the distance, an f-stop over f/11 would be used. The depth of field increases in this case because a smaller aperture opening restricts the beam of light passing through the lens. When this cone of light is concentrated, all the images appear in focus.

With autofocus systems, the camera's software automatically determines the aperture opening. If the AF senses an object is very close, it will open the aperture. If the camera is pointed at objects in the distance, the operating system will close down the aperture.

Light and Shutter Speed

After the camera software chooses the aperture setting, it has to adjust the shutter speed so the photo is not over- or underexposed. This is done by the camera's built-in light meter. Light meters measure the brightness of light in a scene and relay the information to the camera's firmware. Depending on the mode setting, the camera will adjust the aperture, the shutter speed, or both, so that a photograph is properly exposed.

Light meters work in three ways, depending on the camera. The simplest light meters are called center-weighted. These place greater value on the light in the middle of the scene. Spot meters limit the light to a tiny area of the scene and ignore the light around it. Matrix meters break the entire scene into pieces and take readings from those segments. This creates the most accurate overall reading of a scene.

Whatever the type of light meter, it works in conjunction with the aperture. If a low f-stop is used, more light pours into the camera. The light meter will choose a fast shutter speed, such as 1/250th of a second, to prevent overexposure. The opposite is true when a high f-stop is used. In such cases, a longer shutter speed, such as 1/60th of a second, is necessary to properly expose the photo.

Film and ISO Numbers

In the decades before digital photography, each role of film was given an ISO (International Organization for Standardization) number, based on its "speed" or light sensitivity. Film that was less sensitive to light, or slower, had a smaller ISO number. For example, the popular color film Kodachrome was rated ISO 64. Fujicolor Superia was faster and was available in ISO 200, 400, 800, and 1600. These fast films, especially 800 and 1600, were extremely sensitive to light and could be used in darkened rooms or to shoot concerts, fireworks, and nighttime landscapes and cityscapes. Because of the chemical composition of high-speed film, shots appeared with relatively large multicolored specks that were visible to the eye. This was especially true if the photograph was enlarged or cropped. Conversely, slow film provided a fine, small-grain texture that gave photographs higher image quality.

While digital cameras allow photographers to change ISO between every shot, this was not possible during the film era. If a photographer wanted to shoot at a different ISO, it was necessary to change the entire roll of film in the camera. For that reason, some photographers carried several cameras when shooting, each loaded with a different ISO speed film.

ISO Settings

A third setting that can affect aperture and shutter speed is called the ISO. This setting is an acronym for the International Organization for Standardization, based in Geneva, Switzerland, that established the standard. ISO was originally designated to rate the light sensitivity or "speed" of a film. So-called slow film, such as ISO 100, was used on bright, sunny days. Fast film, such as ISO 800, was good for shooting indoors or at dawn or dusk.

The relationship between exposure and film speed changed with the advent of digital photography. Since there is no light-sensitive film being used, the ISO number is applied to the light sensitivity of the image sensor. The lower the ISO rating, the less sensitive the image sensor is to light.

Most digital cameras have standard ISO settings of 100, 200, 400, 800, and automatic. Digital single lens reflex cameras can achieve ISO 1600, 3200, or higher. Each number is double the previous number's light sensitivity. For example, when the ISO is set at 400, the image sensor is twice as sensitive to light as it would be at ISO 200.

Higher ISO settings of 400 or above produce a type of graininess known as noise. These appear as multicolored speckles in the shadows and darker areas of a photograph. Noise is caused because the image sensor is working harder to take a photograph in a low-light setting. According to photographer David Raboin, "At this low range your [photosites] might be measuring a charge created by the heat of the camera rather than a charge created by light striking the sensor. You're at the limits of your sensor's abilities. It can't tell the difference between a good and bad [light] measurement at this range."[4]

High ISO settings result in fuzzy-looking pictures. Color accuracy might be off and fine details lost. High ISO problems are dealt with in several ways. DSLRs have large, powerful image sensors that suppress noise at high ISO. Those with less expensive cameras cannot do much about noise when taking a picture. However, they can reduce noise during the editing process. Almost all photo-editing software has a noise adjustment feature to tone down the odd-color pixels in the shadows.

Auto Mode

When a camera is set on auto mode, it judges focus, reads the light, and automatically sets the aperture, shutter speed, ISO, and focus. The auto mode is represented by a green rectangular icon or camera symbol with "Auto" written on it.

The auto mode is designed for people who simply want to point their camera at a subject and click a picture. The mode provides a sense of freedom to photographers who do not want to worry about the technical details of photography.

Auto mode—indicated by the green box icon on the functions dial of this Canon EOS 40D—sets the camera to automatically handle the aperture, shutter speed, ISO, and focus.

As wedding photographer Natalie Norton explains, "Auto can give you a great opportunity for exploration, frankly because it's less to think about. You have the freedom to 'go out on a limb' artistically speaking that you wouldn't be able to were you going mad metering light, selecting shutter speeds and fiddling with apertures."[5]

Portrait Mode

While the auto mode is the easiest to use, it does not take the best possible pictures when photographing faces and heads, or portraits. Since people and pets are the most popular picture subjects, cameras have a special mode for portraits. It is indicated on the mode dial with an icon of a person's head turned to the side. Portrait mode is used when a single subject fills most of the frame.

As with auto mode, when portrait mode is selected, the camera's sensors and software determine ISO and aperture settings, along with shutter speed. Portrait mode automatically sets the aperture to a large size so that the depth of field is shallow. Background objects will be out of focus and will not compete for attention with the subject being photographed. Portrait mode will select a higher shutter speed to compensate for the wide-open aperture. Because portraits are shot at close range, the flash will be triggered when the photo is taken. This eliminates shadows on the subject's face.

On cameras that have both active and passive autofocus, portrait mode will select the active setting. Experienced photographers aim the autofocus sensor at the eyes for reasons explained by freelance photographer Ibarionex Perello:

In a portrait, nothing is more important than the eyes. The eyes are the very first place we look when looking at an image of a person. As a result, the eyes need to be one of the sharpest elements in the frame. If the eyes aren't in focus, the viewer's experience of the photograph can be diminished. . . . Controlling which AF sensors are used is particularly important if you're using a wide aperture that can result in a very narrow depth of field. Otherwise, the camera could focus on the nose or the shirt, which could result in the eyes being slightly soft, which you always want to avoid.[6]

Landscape Mode

Landscape photography is the opposite of portraiture in most ways. The photographer wants everything in the scene to be in sharp focus. The landscape mode is indicated on the camera by an icon representing a mountain. In this setting, a small aperture will be selected to increase the depth of field. Lower ISO settings, between 100 and 200, will provide a smooth, high-resolution shot with little noise.

The light meter will automatically set a slow shutter speed to compensate for the high aperture setting. However, the photographer must be prepared if the shutter speed is 1/30th of a second or longer. At slow shutter speeds, the entire image might appear blurry or shaken, because it is almost impossible to hold a camera perfectly still; people breathe and their hands naturally tremble to a small degree. For this reason, photographers use three-legged camera stands called tripods.

A man photographs the Ganges range in Nepal using a telephoto lens and a DSLR camera mounted on a tripod. Digital cameras typically offer a landscape mode that reduces the aperture and increases the depth of field.

A camera mounted on a tripod is stabilized and will provide the sharpest possible photographs. Tripods are also useful for photographers shooting with heavy lenses. As landscape photographer Fred Hanselmann explains, "With the 28mm to 70mm zoom lens attached, [my camera] weighs almost eight pounds [3.6kg]. This is a lot of camera to hold up to your eye for a long period of time searching for just the right composition."[7]

Sports Mode

Tripods are also used when shooting in sports mode, indicated on the mode dial by an icon of a runner. Sports mode is useful for action shots. The camera choses a fast shutter speed of around 1/1000th of a second. This setting is essential for freezing action in the photo. With fast shutter speeds, a wider aperture is used. This gives many sports photos a shallow depth of field. High ISO speeds of up to 800 are usually selected for sports photography.

In an action photo shot with a shutter speed of 1/60th of a second, the photographer can move the camera lens to follow a subject as it moves. This process is called panning. If a photographer pans a race car zipping around a track, the car will be in focus while the background is a sweeping blur. This gives the photo a feeling of speed.

Night Scene

A tripod is necessary when using a camera's night scene mode. This mode is indicated on the dial by a black square around a white star and a graphic of a person's head and

In sports mode, digital cameras use very fast shutter speed of around 1/1000th of a second to freeze action.

Working with Aperture Settings

Photographer David D. Busch explains how cameras change shutter speeds to compensate for a manually selected aperture setting:

You're shooting a soccer game outdoors with a telephoto lens [for example] and want a relatively high shutter speed but you don't care if the speed changes a little should the sun duck behind a cloud. Set your camera to A or Av, and adjust the aperture until a shutter speed of, say, 1/1000th of a second is selected at your current ISO setting. Then go ahead and shoot, knowing that your camera will maintain that f/11 aperture (for sufficient depth-of-field as the soccer players move around the field), but will drop down to 1/750th or 1/500th [of a] second if necessary should the light change a little.

David D. Busch. *Digital SLR Photography*. Boston: Course Technology, 2012, p. 59.

shoulders. Night scene is designed for taking landscape or cityscape photographs, or anywhere there is not enough natural light. The setting is used right after sunset, at night, before dawn, or indoors where low-lighting conditions are present.

When night scene mode is used, the shutter speed is slowed to around 1/15th of second. The flash ignites, but this often lights up unwanted subject matter close to the camera, which detracts from the photograph. For example, if night scene mode is used to shoot a band playing music in a concert hall, the flash will only illuminate the people sitting directly in front of the photographer. The band will appear insignificant in the photo. In such cases, the photographer can choose to turn off the flash manually. Another problem with night scene is that the camera selects the highest ISO, which can result in noise and inaccurate colors.

Night Portrait Mode

Another low-light setting, night portrait mode, is indicated by an icon with a crescent moon above a person's head. As the mode's name indicates, it is used to shoot portraits at night. When properly executed, night portrait mode will evenly expose details of subjects in the foreground and nighttime scenes in the background.

When set in night portrait mode, the aperture is half-closed, which gives good depth of field. The shutter speed is also in the middle range. Usually the flash is triggered, but on some cameras, night scene mode works without a flash. When the shutter release button is pushed, the camera takes

several photographs in very rapid succession at different exposure levels. The camera software then blends the images to create one evenly exposed shot.

Macro Mode

Barely visible objects can make stunning pictures when photographed extremely close up with a camera's macro mode. While the best effects can be achieved with a macro lens on a DSLR, most point-and-shoot cameras have good macro capabilities and do not require expensive lenses.

The macro mode is indicated by a flower icon. This setting allows the camera's lens to focus on objects that are very close, between 2 and 32 inches (5 and 81cm) from the camera. Macro mode is good for photographing objects smaller than a hand. If the photographer wants to shoot very small subjects, such as insects, a special close-up lens is necessary.

In macro, the camera opens the aperture to its widest setting, which provides the shallowest depth of field; ISO

This photo of a ladybug shows the extreme close-up possible with macro mode, a common feature in point-and-shoot digital cameras. DSLR cameras can be outfitted with macro lenses for more extreme detail.

settings are low. When working in macro, the flash often triggers automatically because of the low level of light between the camera and the subject. In some cases, this results in an overexposed, washed-out picture that does not capture interesting details. In these instances, the flash can be turned off manually.

Manual-enable Modes

Many cameras allow the photographer to bypass the various pre-set modes and manually select settings to fine-tune their exposures. Manual settings allow photographers more freedom to shoot in extreme conditions. For example, a very bright scene such as a snow-covered mountain can fool the camera's automatic setting, causing it to choose a very fast shutter speed that would underexpose the photo. This would produce gray snow rather than white. The reverse is true when shooting dark scenes indoors or outside at night; the auto setting would chose a very large aperture opening that could overexpose the picture and make it appear washed out and lacking in contrast. Manual controls allow photographers to fine-tune the settings to prevent such problems.

Photographers who wish to manually adjust the aperture can set the mode dial on one of two settings, A or AV. The A symbol stands for aperture and AV stands for aperture value. Both indicate the same thing, aperture priority. With aperture priority, photographers can manually adjust a photo's depth of field.

To use aperture priority, photographers choose from a menu of f-stops listed on the LCD. When a specific aperture is selected, the light meter will compensate with a shutter speed that is appropriate for the shooting conditions.

Photographers can manually select the shutter speed with either the S or TV setting. S stands for shutter, and TV stands for time value. Both symbols indicate shutter priority. Fast shutter speeds ensure razor-sharp photos no matter how unsteady the photographer's hands. Slow shutter speeds—under 1/15th of a second—blur movement, which can be used for artistic effect. For example, shooting a photo of a waterfall, river, or waves with a slow shutter gives the water a pleasing, gauzy effect.

Photographers who want to set both aperture and shutter speed separately can select the M, or manual, setting. This setting might be used when shooting moving subjects at night, such as bicyclists on a city street. The photographer could stop the action with a fast shutter, but open the aperture very wide to achieve a proper exposure. On the other hand, the photograph could use a slow shutter speed to give the bicyclists a blurry sense of speed, while shutting down the aperture to give a sharper depth of field.

On some cameras, the LCD will display the manual settings alongside the settings the camera would have automatically selected. This allows the photographer to keep the manual settings within a range that will still guarantee decent shots.

Smartphone Software Apps

Smartphones allow users to download numerous photography applications, or apps. Some of the most popular apps are filters that make digital photos look like they were shot on film. Effects include antique, sepia, black and white, and negative. Some filters give photos the washed-out colors of photographs taken in the 1950s and 1960s. Filters also can add unusual effects to make photos look like crumpled paper or comic book drawings. Several apps can change the eye color of a subject. There are also photography apps to reduce graininess, fix under- or overexposed images, and straighten crooked shots.

Specialized Modes

In general, the more a camera costs, the more modes it will have, and some DSLRs have highly specialized modes. One of the best modes for shooting outdoors is called stitch assist, or photostitch. This is indicated by an icon on the dial resembling several overlapping rectangular pictures. When in stitch assist mode, the photographer can shoot multiple photographs in quick succession, moving the camera slightly for every shot. The camera's firmware then combines the images into a single panoramic picture that can include a full circular view.

To capture this image of a waterfall with the moving water in a blur, the photographer used a slow shutter speed. A water mode on many digital cameras can be used to achieve a similar effect.

Fireworks mode is used when a camera is on a tripod. It shoots an extended exposure of about four seconds to capture fireworks as they streak across the sky. Water mode works in two ways. It can be set to freeze the movement of water with a high shutter speed or the opposite, capturing the fuzzy motion of water with a slow speed shutter. Special scene mode, or SCN, allows photographers to choose from a menu of settings meant for a variety of special conditions. Special scene settings may include snowy mountains, beaches, indoors, and foliage.

Complicated and Easy

Mode settings make complicated calculations based on light, movement, and distance. Before digital cameras, these tasks involved guesswork and a good understanding of camera mechanisms. With modern digital cameras, photography is easy for amateurs, while those with more advanced skills can customize their shots. Photographers can shoot a scene in multiple modes and choose the best shot without the worry of ruining expensive film. From auto to manual, digital camera modes present a broad range of choices to photographers and ensure that every subject is presented in the best light.

CHAPTER 3

Camcorders vs. Still Cameras

The mode dials on most digital cameras include an icon of a little video camera. When the video setting is used, the camera switches from taking still pictures to making movies. The video option is also available on most smartphones, computer tablets, and even some MP3 players. Although most of these devices shoot fairly good videos, that is not their main purpose. Stand-alone video camera recorders, or camcorders, were specifically designed for shooting videos and generally make better movies than smartphones, tablets, or MP3 players.

Compared to smartphones and point-and-shoot still cameras, camcorders feature higher-resolution lenses, record better-quality sound, and employ anti-shaking capabilities not found on other devices. Camcorders are also designed to store large video files, some up to two hours long. This compares favorably to most still cameras, which can only shoot videos of less than thirty minutes. Even the highest-quality DSLRs are limited to film clips of twelve to twenty-three minutes depending on image quality.

Camcorder and Camera Similarities

In most basic ways, camcorders and still cameras function in a similar fashion. Both rely on lenses, apertures, and shutters to transmit light to image sensors. The photons of light are turned into electronic signals after passing through an analog-to-digital converter.

Like a digital camera, a camcorder uses computer chips and software programs to focus, adjust the aperture and shutter, and store images and sounds as digital data on a memory device. Also similar to digital cameras, camcorders have viewfinders and LCD screens that can also be used for watching stored videos and scrolling through various options. Most camcorder LCDs are of the tilt and twist variety.

Quiet, Steady Zooms

One of the major differences between camcorders and still cameras concerns lenses. As a basic rule of photography, the bigger and heavier the lens, the better the image quality. For that reason, the small lenses on point-and-shoot still cameras, tablet cameras, and smartphone cameras cannot match the resolution of the larger lenses on most stand-alone camcorders.

Similar to digital cameras, camcorders also have viewfinders, LCD screens, and software programs for exposure settings.

In addition to larger lenses, camcorders are designed with optical zooms, which are much higher quality than the digital zooms found on smartphones and other digital cameras. Optical zooms physically move within the lens to make distant objects appear closer. Standard camcorders have a 10x zoom, while some with ultra-optical zooms are rated as 18x or 35x.

When a camcorder zooms in and out, the movement can be seen in real time on the video. Jittery, jumpy zooms can make viewers feel dizzy or seasick. Since zoom shots need to be extremely smooth and steady, camcorder controls are designed to provide the most sensitive lens movement possible.

When a camcorder operator presses the zoom button on the outer case, it activates a set of complex, finely tuned zoom motors inside the lens. These work to glide the lens back and forth. Unlike the loud, buzzing motors on still cameras, camcorder zoom motors are very quiet. This prevents what is called zoom motor whine, which could be recorded by the camcorder's microphones.

Camcorder lenses also feature advanced image stabilizers. Still cameras have image stabilizers, too, but they are only designed to counteract hand movement for the split second when the shutter is open. Camcorders are designed for operators who might be walking, crouching, or even running. Stabilizers can prevent scenes from looking like they were shot in an earthquake. Photography educator Steve Sanders explains:

> Image stabilization is an important, yet overlooked feature on digital camcorders. It's designed to eliminate a shaky image caused by a shaky camera. Shaky cameras can be caused by a few different things. The biggest culprit is shooting hand held, but even if you are using a tripod you can suffer from the shakes too. Anytime you touch the camera provides an opportunity for your shot to suffer, like when you're hitting the record button. Shakes are even more extreme when zooming because a little shake becomes magnified.[8]

Camcorder image stabilizers come in optical and digital form, with optical systems considered superior. Camcorders with optical image stabilization have a mini gyroscope inside the lens called a microelectromechanical system (MEMS). Like a toy gyroscope, or top, these devices maintain balance by spinning rapidly. Unlike toys, the MEMS is highly sophisticated and very small.

The complex MEMS employs a pair of special sensors that can detect the movement or rotation of the camera. When movement is detected, a microcontroller directs signals to small, sensitive motors attached to the image sensor and the lens. The motors move the lens and image sensor very slightly to counteract shaking. Similar systems are used to trigger automobile airbags at the moment of impact when an accident occurs.

Shooting Movies with a DSLR

Most still cameras do not have the movie-making capabilities of standard camcorders. However, in the 2010s, independent filmmakers discovered that the Canon 7D DSLR exceeded the quality of camcorders—and even professional movie cameras.

The Canon 7D costs around $1,500, which is much less expensive than professional movie cameras that begin at $20,000. The 7D's quality is provided by one of the largest image sensors on the market. This gives the movies shot with the Canon a cinematic quality not found in typical cameras. Filmmaker Mike Figgis explains:

> [The 7D is] one of the major breakthroughs in cinematic technology of the last 100 years. . . . If you use the right lenses you can completely emulate the shallow depth of field that a cinema lens gives you, which everybody, whether or not they know anything about film, recognizes instinctively as looking like cinema. Whereas with video you always have this horrific, massive depth of field where everything's in focus.

When compared to a standard camcorder, the 7D has one major drawback. It can only record twelve minutes of high-definition footage or twenty-three minutes using standard-definition settings. Even the cheapest camcorders can store one hour's worth of footage.

Quoted in "Canon EOS7D: A New Lens on the Scene." *The Independent*, February 23, 2011. www.independent.co.uk/life-style/gadgets-and-tech/features/canon-eos-7d-a-new-lens-on-the-scene-2222887.html.

Camcorders with optical image stabilization are typically bigger, more expensive, and use more battery power than those with digital image stabilizers. Digital image stabilizers are smaller, cheaper, and lighter. They work with software that analyzes single frames of video and compares the placement of images to detect shaking. If there is a major difference

The Rise and Fall of Flip

As more people started to use smartphones to shoot videos, camcorder sales plunged in the 2010s. One of the biggest camcorder flops during this era was the Flip Video HD. When the Flip was first marketed in 2007 for $150, it was instantly popular. In its first year, the Flip became the top-selling camcorder on Amazon.com and captured 13 percent of the camcorder market. The battery-powered Flip was easy to use, came in bright colors, and could hold up to two hours of video. In 2009, at the height of the Flip fad, the company was purchased for $590 million by the Internet equipment manufacturer Cisco Systems. Two years later, Cisco announced it was shutting down its Flip camcorder division because of weak sales. Within a few years, the Flip went from being one of the most popular camcorder models in the world to being seen as obsolete and outdated.

between two frames, which indicate vibrations, the software discards the pixels that produce the shaking images.

High Definition

Image stabilization is especially important on high-definition (HD) camcorders. These devices utilize digital technology to produce high-resolution, clear images and higher-quality sound.

High definition is a sophisticated system in which the image sensor records nearly seven times as many pixels as a standard-definition (SD) camcorder. High-definition devices are defined by two complex standards: 1280 x 720 or 1920 x 1080. The numbers, which are also used to define HD televisions (HDTVs), refer to the amount of pixel lines the device records. The first, larger number is the width of the image, the smaller number is the height. The numbers are multiplied to determine the number of pixels in each video frame; 1280 x 720 mode contains 921,600 pixels per frame, while 1920 x 1080 contains 2,073,600. By comparison, SD camcorders are defined as 640 x 480; they contain 307,200 pixels per frame.

Whatever the technical definition, HD camcorder prices have fallen dramatically since the first ones were introduced in 2003. Early HD models by Sony, Canon, JVC, and Sharp cost more than $1,500. By 2013, the price of a basic HD camcorder had fallen to around $250. In 2013, three-quarters of all households in the United States had at least one HDTV. With so many people possessing televisions capable of displaying HD videos, camcorders with HD image sensors were among the top-selling models.

Storing Movies on Mini Cassettes

Whether a camcorder is HD or SD, video files need to be stored within the device until they are transferred to a computer hard drive, DVD, or uploaded to the Internet. Until around 2010, MiniDV (digital video) cassettes were the main video storage method for camcorders. The inexpensive mini cassettes hold almost thirteen gigabytes of information, which translates to sixty minutes of standard-definition video.

MiniDV cassettes use .25-inch (6.35mm) metal magnetic tape to record very high-quality digital video. The tapes load directly into the camcorder. When videos are shot, the information captured by the lens and image sensor is sent directly to the tape for storage. Once a video is recorded on a MiniDV cassette, it can be transferred to the computer in real time. That is, a sixty-minute movie takes sixty minutes to download. The transfer is done through a DV cable that connects to a FireWire terminal, also known as an IEEE 1394 port, located on computers and camcorders.

MiniDVs have some disadvantages. Like old audiocassettes and VHS tapes, the tape can break or get tangled, and the mechanical parts of the cassettes wear out. In addition, the cassettes can only be played on MiniDV camcorders, which also wear out and break.

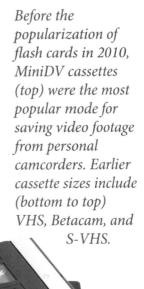

Before the popularization of flash cards in 2010, MiniDV cassettes (top) were the most popular mode for saving video footage from personal camcorders. Earlier cassette sizes include (bottom to top) VHS, Betacam, and S-VHS.

Flash Cards

While most camera makers continued to produce MiniDV camcorders in the 2010s, the popularity of the format plummeted as cassettes were replaced by flash memory cards. Flash memory cards are superior to MiniDV cassettes, as they are light and compact and contain no moving parts. With MiniDVs, a camcorder user might need to carry two or three bulky cassettes on vacation. A similar number of flash cards takes up less room than a pack of gum. In addition, the memory cards store videos as complete files. The cards can be inserted into a card reader that is plugged into a computer. The files can be dragged and dropped, or transferred, to the computer in a few minutes, much like music or photo files.

By 2013, more than two hundred camcorder models stored videos on flash memory cards. Standard-definition camcorders, which produce about one gigabyte of video per hour, require SD flash cards. High-definition camcorders create about ten gigabytes of video per hour. In addition, these files are created at a rapid rate of speed. As such, HD camcorders require a newer type of flash card called SDXC, which is faster. This format is much more expensive. For example, in 2013 a 64GB SDXC cost around $500, nearly ten times the cost of an SD card with similar capacity.

Mics and Sound

Storage media must also record audio tracks that accompany videos. When it comes to sound quality, camcorders have several clear advantages over still cameras. While both types of cameras have built-in microphones (mics), camcorders feature microphone jacks. This allows users to plug external microphones into the device. These external mics generally provide better sound quality, as camera reviewer Josh Lehrer explains: "Using an external microphone is ideal especially when recording video outside, and even a cheap external microphone can take your video to the next level."[9]

There are several types of external mics that are designed for specific users. Lavalier microphones are fastened to clothing with a clip, pin, or magnet. These are often worn by guests in talk show settings. A long, cylindrical mic called a shotgun microphone excels at picking up soft sounds and can be used by those shooting videos of birds or small animals. Shotgun mics are designed to record the human voice and are used by news reporters and others speaking in front of a camcorder.

Microphone jacks can also be used to plug in camcorder XLR adapters. These are small, lightweight sound boxes, like a mixing board, that enable users to attach two microphones directly to the camcorder. The sound levels of each mic can be adjusted independently. XLR adapters have headphone jacks with volume controls. Camcorder XLR adapters upgrade and expand the audio capabilities of a basic camcorder to the level of a professional movie camera.

A shotgun microphone, such as this one mounted on a DSLR camera, is an external microphone used to pick up subtle atmospheric sounds and clear voice recordings.

With all their sound, memory, and video capabilities, camcorders consume much more power than still cameras, which run on inexpensive AA batteries or small rechargeable lithium-ion batteries. Most camcorders have large rechargeable lithium-ion battery packs that provide power for about one hour. In addition, most camcorders can be plugged into conventional AC power outlets.

Camcorder Modes

While battery and sound capabilities set camcorders apart from still cameras, both types of cameras feature similar shooting modes, such as portrait, sports, night, fireworks, and manual. Like still cameras, camcorder modes work by adjusting aperture, shutter, and autofocus settings. Also, while still cameras can shoot in video mode, camcorders have photo mode for shooting still photographs. This will allow the operator to either shoot a single photo or freeze a frame of a video. However, the image quality in most camcorders is lower because it was not designed for use as a still camera.

Some camcorders have specialized modes that compensate for the movement of the camera and operator. For example, Panasonic offers users a mode called O.I.S., which stands for optical image stabilization. More than a standard stabilizer, this feature allows users to lock onto a subject by touching its image on the camcorder's LCD screen. As a video is shot, the O.I.S. keeps the moving object in focus.

Like still cameras, many camcorders have a face detection mode that works through the autofocus system. Steve Sanders explains how camcorder face detection works:

> Face detection is a special type of auto focus mode which doesn't focus on everything. This is able to differentiate between people's faces and any other objects. The faces will be locked onto even if they are not in the center of the frame. . . . Most camcorders support multiple face detection, which makes it possible to select many faces rather than just one. . . . The best video cameras are capable of detecting 20+ faces which should be plenty for most people.[10]

Going Wireless

In the 2010s, as the video quality of smartphones continued to improve, people increasingly used their phones to shoot movies. As economic analyst Brent Bracelin stated, "It's a testament to the pace of innovation in consumer electronics and smartphone technology. More and more functionality is being integrated into smartphones."[11] In order to compete with easy-to-use smartphones, camcorder manufacturers began featuring the Wi-Fi option.

With Wi-Fi, users can wirelessly transfer SD or HD videos from their camcorders to a computer. The camcorders can also work with other devices, such as monitors, televisions, or media players, attached to a Wi-Fi network. This means videos can be streamed directly from a camcorder to viewing devices without wire cables.

While Wi-Fi camcorders allow users to "cut the cable," there are some disadvantages. Wi-Fi camcorders do not have direct access to the Internet like smartphones. This means a user cannot upload videos directly to a social networking or video-sharing site. In addition, large files, especially HD movies, take much longer to transfer wirelessly, while the process is a big drain on the camcorder battery if no AC power is available.

Sports Camcorders

Despite extra features such as Wi-Fi, camcorder sales plunged 43 percent between 2011 and 2012. However, this trend did not affect the growing popularity of sports camcorders, first introduced in 2011. Sports camcorders are compact, "wearable" devices that can be mounted on

Sports camcorders, such as this "hatcam" designed by PBS to collect live footage in 2012, use a Go-Pro camera and a shotgun microphone mounted on a helmet.

The First Helmet Cam

In the 2010s, sports camcorders made by GoPro or Sony were made to be mounted on the helmets of cyclists, skiers, football players, and other athletes. These cameras, batteries included, weighed only 3.3 ounces (94g), less than the average smartphone. The first cyclist to use a helmet camcorder had to contend with much more weight.

One of the earliest helmet cams was invented in 1987 by cyclist Mark Schulze, who mounted a color video camera to a motorcycle helmet. During this era, the camera had to be hard-wired to a separate VHS portable video recorder, which was nearly the size of a microwave oven. Schulze carried the recorder in a backpack along with a heavy lead-acid battery. With all this bulky equipment, the first helmet cam weighed more than 20 pounds (9kg). Despite the heavy equipment, Schulze used his helmet cam to film *The Great Mountain Biking Video*, which can still be seen on YouTube.

helmets, diving masks, headbands, wristbands, and chest harnesses.

The sports camcorder concept was popularized by GoPro, founded by surfer Nick Woodman in 2004. Woodman raised money to found the company selling $20 handmade beaded belts out of his Volkswagen van.

GoPro HD camcorders are simple and small. They weigh around 3.3 ounces (94g) with their rechargeable lithium-ion battery. GoPro is operated by a small, wireless remote control that allows users to activate or stop the record function. The camcorders lack LCD screens but have Wi-Fi. This allows them to connect with a smartphone or tablet running the GoPro app. The app lets users review videos and acts as a control for camcorder features.

The GoPro is enclosed in a clear plastic housing that is shockproof and waterproof. The housing is designed to latch on to special GoPro mounts that are made for a variety of situations. Suction cups are used to mount the camcorders on race cars and other vehicles; handlebar mounts are used on bicycles; and surfboard mounts are available for surfers.

As the sports camcorder fad exploded, Sony, JVC, and other manufacturers introduced their own sports camcorder models. However, GoPro led the market, selling more than 3 million camcorders between 2011 and 2012. By 2013, there were more than 10 million individually shot GoPro videos on YouTube. According to market analyst Tim Peterson, "GoPro's YouTube channel—which counts more than 208 million video views—is full of brand- and user-generated videos, be it swimming tigers from the Australia Zoo, a backboard view of a college basketball player's dunk or Porter, 'the world's first driving dog'—all appended with some variation of 'shot on my GoPro.'"[12]

3-D Camcorders

Another type of camcorder, which shoots 3-D videos, was introduced around the same time as GoPro. The camcorders were designed to take advantage of the growing interest in 3-D television sets, which were introduced in 2010.

Three-dimensional videos provide the illusion of depth. Images seem to jump off the screen and hover directly in front of the faces of viewers wearing special 3-D glasses with one red lens and one cyan (greenish-blue) lens. The 3-D impression is created by the camcorder, which uses two lenses to record separate left and right images. These can be viewed on 3-D televisions with the red-and-cyan glasses. The use of two lenses does impose some limits on 3-D camcorders. They generally need bright light and are more sensitive to shaking than regular camcorders.

The addition of 3-D is one more way camcorder manufacturers have tried to stay relevant in the age of point-and-shoot cameras, cell phones, and tablets, which perform many of the functions of a camcorder. However, even this move might not keep stand-alone camcorders relevant in

HOW 3-D IMAGES ARE CAPTURED AND PROJECTED

Each eye sees with a slight difference in perspective. The brain uses the two different views to create the impression of three-dimensional space.

To record in 3-D, cameras film from two perspectives, mimicking human sight.

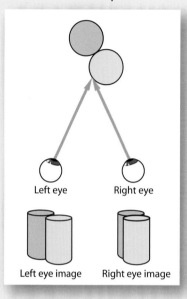

Left eye   Right eye

Left eye image   Right eye image

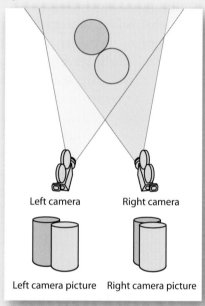

Left camera   Right camera

Left camera picture   Right camera picture

To see the image or movie in 3-D, the left eye gets the view of the left camera and the right eye gets the view of the right camera. The brain combines the two images into a single 3-D image.

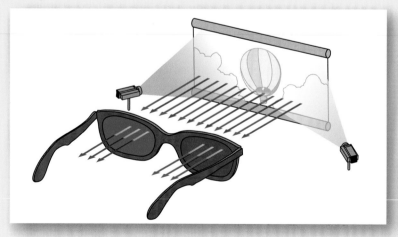

the future. Advanced 3-D technology was made available on smartphones in 2011, with the introduction of the HTC EVO 3D and the LG Optimus 3D.

Whatever the current trends or fads, there is little doubt that stand-alone camcorders are some of the most advanced high-tech consumer items ever invented. While dozens of devices can now shoot short videos, camcorders continue to offer the most features and the highest-quality images. The task of manufacturers is to convince consumers that these tools are necessary. Unless they do, the camcorder might be obsolete within a few years.

CHAPTER 4

The Digital Darkroom

Before the era of digital cameras, consumers sent their rolls of film to photo labs. Within a few hours or days they received an envelope filled with 3 x 5-inch (7.6 x 12.7cm) photos. For most, this was the end of the photography process. Pictures that were under- or overexposed, out of focus, or not well-framed were thrown out or tossed in a box and forgotten. There might be a few photos that were good enough to reproduce and share with friends and relatives. Doing so required another trip to the photo lab, where a film negative could be enlarged to 5 x 7 inches (12.7 x 17.7cm), 8 x 10 inches (20.3 x 25.4cm), or 11 x 14 inches (28 x 35cm).

Those with a greater interest in film photography had options beyond the photo lab. They could set up a darkroom and fill it with trays of chemicals, photosensitive paper, an enlarger, and other items. These tools allowed photographers to crop images, fix bad exposures, enhance contrast, and perform a host of other tasks using a negative. During the film era, most people did not bother with darkrooms; they required expensive equipment, large sinks, temperature-controlled water, and special red "safelights" that would not expose the photographic paper.

Most who did have darkrooms usually only worked in black and white. The task of printing color photographs was even more complex and expensive. And whether the photographer worked in black and white or color, darkroom photo printing was time-consuming. It required patience, practice, and skill. The rewards for this persistence came with the ability to produce artistic, one-of-a-kind prints. As Ansel Adams wrote, "The making of a print is a unique combination of mechanical execution and creative activity. . . . Just as different photographers can interpret one subject in numerous ways, depending on personal vision, so might they each make varying prints from identical negatives."[13]

Darkroom Hardware

Since the demise of the film era, the darkroom has gone digital. Chemicals, trays, safelights, and enlargers have been replaced by digital hardware such as computers and monitors. Creative photo editing that once required a high degree of technical skill can be done on a PC, laptop, tablet, smartphone, or the digital camera itself.

Once the photographer is satisfied with a picture, it can be reproduced cheaply and easily with a photo printer. As camera reviewer Amadou Diallo states, "There are few things more satisfying than seeing your image on paper

Instead of a darkroom, a contemporary photographer's workspace is an office with a monitor, a computer with editing software, a scanner, and a printer.

Photo Printers

For those who wish to hang their photographs on the wall or display them in a picture frame, a photo printer is an essential tool for the digital darkroom. Most photo printers are of the inkjet variety. They spray droplets of ink through a printhead that moves from left to right across the print surface. Printheads contain tiny openings called nozzles that spray dots that are so small they are measured in units called picoliters, which are one trillionth of a liter (33.9 ounces). The nozzles adjust the size and spacing of the dots to produce various tones. Dots that are tightly packed together will produce darker areas than those that are spaced farther apart. A motor in the printer advances the print paper line by line. Blank areas are exposed to the ink-firing nozzles. The placement of the dots is controlled by software that can produce millions of colors. Specially coated paper maintains image sharpness by preventing the ink dots from spreading into one another.

as a finished print. Current technology has made producing exhibition-quality prints from the comfort of your own home easier than ever before."[14]

The scanner is another important piece of hardware for the digital darkroom. Scanners are inexpensive tools that convert old film photographs to digital files. These can be edited in much the same manner as photographs from a digital camera. Scanners come in a variety of styles. Pass-through scanners are designed so users can feed their photographs into the device. As the image moves through the device on rubber rollers, it is scanned and the photo files are stored on a built-in memory card. Slide scanners are specially calibrated to work with 35mm reversal film, a photographic film that created positive images, rather than negatives. Reversal film was mounted on square frames called slides that could be viewed with a slide projector. During the film era, slides were preferred by some because they had better contrast and higher image resolution when compared to negatives. Slides and slide projectors were also the best way to show photographs to large groups of people, whether in an auditorium or a living room.

Photo-Editing Software

Whatever hardware is found in a digital darkroom, it is controlled by powerful software. These applications allow photographers to acquire images from a scanner or camera, manage those images, and edit, print, and upload them to the Web.

Some photo-editing programs can be downloaded free from the Internet, others cost hundreds of dollars and offer specialized functions designed for professional photographers. Whatever the price, all photo-editing software performs a menu of basic tasks. Users can adjust tone, contrast, and sharpness, and resize, crop, and rotate photographs. Most software offers quick fixes to enhance photos with the click of a mouse. There are also numerous filters and special effects that can be used to turn average photographs into unique artworks. Some of the more advanced applications have tools for combining multiple photos, adding text, and adjusting colors with extreme precision.

Adjusting Pixels

Most photo-editing software applications, including Adobe Photoshop, Picasa, Aperture, and GIMP, are pixel-based; they work by manipulating pixels. Each pixel has a specific brightness and color that relates to what is called the red, green, and blue, or RGB, color system. Red, green, and blue are the primary colors of light. This means that every color the human eye perceives is some combination of red, green, and blue light. For example, when a person sees a yellow leaf, the leaf is actually reflecting a combination of red and green light to produce the color yellow. The pinkish-purple color magenta is a mix of red and blue. Orange is two parts

*Photo-editing
programs, such as
Adobe Photoshop,
use mathematical
algorithms and
a variety of user-
controlled tools
to manipulate the
pixels of images.*

red light and one part green. (The RGB system differs from the way paint colors are mixed, for example, by making orange from yellow and red.)

Photo-editing software changes the color of each pixel in a photograph by altering the various percentages, or values, of red, green, and blue in any color. Pixels can also be made brighter or darker. All changes are determined by complex mathematical formulas, called algorithms, within the editing application.

While the technical details are complicated, most applications make photo editing simple with automatic adjustments. These options are instantly applied globally—that is, over the entire area of the photo. One of the most basic automatic improvements, called either auto tone, vibrancy, or enhance, changes a photograph's color and brightness. This option is used when an image lacks contrast or color brilliance, or is too dark. Photos with these problems are often shot under overcast skies or in low light.

The automatic enhance button globally increases the richness of the color in a photo without making it overwhelmingly bright. The effect works when the software analyzes the lightest and darkest parts of a photo. It boosts pixel color and brightness values in the shadow areas of the scene.

Other common fixes are not done globally but on specific areas of a photograph. The red-eye fix is used to correct a problem caused by flashbulbs used at close range in low light. The flash reflects off the blood vessel on the inner part of the eyeball, and causes the subject to appear with bright red pupils.

When the red-eye fix is clicked, the mouse pointer on the computer screen turns into a little circle with crosshairs. The user drags the circle over the red eye and clicks the mouse button. The photo-editing program automatically turns the selected red pixels to black. Red eyes can also be fixed manually when the user selects a paintbrush tool with the mouse and uses it to paint over the red with black. This requires a steady, practiced hand, which is why many photographers prefer the automatic red-eye fix.

The blemish-removal feature is similar to the red-eye fix but is used to remove pimples or other skin imperfections on portraits. The blemish fix also can be used to remove scratches and dust marks on a photo caused by a dirty camera lens or image sensor. When using the blemish-removal tool, the circle and crosshairs are placed over the problem area, and the software replaces the problem dots, scratches, or blemishes with the correct colored pixels copied from the surrounding area.

BITS & BYTES
DPI
Dots per inch is the resolution measurement for printed images.

Cropping and Straightening

Once colors are satisfactory and blemishes and red eyes are removed, a photographer might chose to reframe, or crop, a picture. This is done to emphasize a specific portion of a photo or eliminate distracting background images.

The crop tool places a movable box, or crop overlay, on top of a photograph. The mouse is placed on the borders of the box, which are moved to create the desired frame around the image. When the crop is applied, the editing software eliminates the unwanted pixels on the outside of the box. After an image is cropped, the remaining image zooms to fill the screen. Photos can be cropped tightly, which brings the edges of the image closer to the subject. Loose cropping shows more of the surroundings and makes the main subject smaller within the frame.

Once a photo is cropped, it is often necessary to straighten the image. The straightening tool is used if the horizon line is not fairly parallel to the bottom of the photo. In addition, vertical subjects, such as tall buildings or lampposts, can sometimes appear tilted. When the straighten option is picked, the pixels are globally rotated with the mouse or the user's fingers on a touch screen. During the process, small areas along the edges of the photo might be eliminated.

Exposure Control

Once a photo is cropped and straightened, photographers can use powerful manual controls to alter the entire look of a photo. The controls are most often sliders that appear in the monitor—bars with buttons in slots that can be moved to increase or decrease various levels.

One of the most basic manual adjustments is used to globally correct the overall exposure of a photograph that is too dark or too light. The brightness slider can either increase or decrease the brightness values of all pixels. The shadow slider works to increase brightness only in the dark areas of a photograph, providing better detail in shadows. The highlight control decreases the brightness values of pixels in bright areas. It is often used to dim down skies so that wispy clouds appear visible.

The contrast tool globally evaluates the contrast, or difference between the light and dark pixels of a photo. Too little contrast will make a photo look flat. Too much contrast will give subjects a sharp, harsh appearance. When contrast is increased, dark pixels are made darker, and light ones become brighter. When contrast is decreased, the difference between light and dark areas is reduced.

MANIPULATING COLOR USING TEMPERATURE AND TINT CONTROLS

All hues of visible light have unique temperatures, distributed as shown on this chart. Image colors can be changed along two axes: Temperature for hues from blue to red and tint for hues from green to magenta.

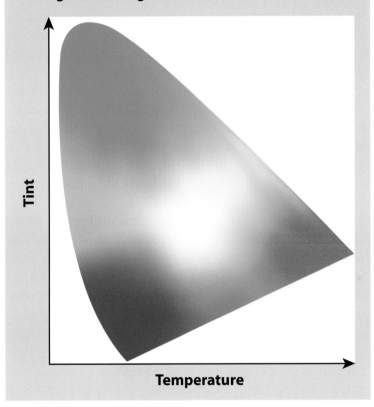

Tint

Temperature

Tint and Temperature

The sliders that govern individual color adjustments are known as tint and temperature. These are used to bring out specific colors or tone them down. The temperature slider is based on color temperature, a system that applies degrees of heat to various light sources. Candles, sunrises and sunsets, and household lights are hot; their color temperature is red.

Light from a clear blue sky is cool, or blue. Camera flash-bulbs and the midday sun fall in the middle temperature range, which is yellow. The temperature slider works with colors ranging from blue to yellowish-orange. The temperature of the pixels that make up these colors can be increased to cool down a photo or increased to give it warmth.

The tint slider covers the rest of the color spectrum, from magenta to green. Tint and temperature settings can make the grass greener and the sea bluer. These controls can decrease colors to give photos an old-fashioned, washed-out look like photos from the 1950s. When pushed to the most extreme settings, tint and temperature controls can create artistic photographs with bright, unearthly hues unlike any produced in a traditional darkroom.

More complex photo editors, such as Adobe Lightroom, include three controls called hue, saturation, and luminance. These features act on specific colors, including red, orange, yellow, green, aqua, blue purple, and magenta. Hue is used to increase or decrease levels of individual colors, while saturation pumps up color levels to provide density or purity of color.

Luminance works the same way that lens filters do. When added to a lens, polarizing filters reduce glare from the sun, ultraviolet (UV) filters make photos look brighter, and other filters add warmth or coolness. The luminance feature has the same effect as these filters, except that it is applied to photos that have already been taken. If a photographer has a picture of flowers in a field on an overcast day, for example, the luminance feature can add a warm glow to the scene.

Slight movement of any color sliders can cause drastic changes to the image. Most people use these controls to make colors look more realistic, but they can also be used for fun. Faces can be turned ghastly hues of green and trees can be made to appear bright pink.

Noise Reduction

When photos have a rough, grainy texture and random spots of color that seem out of place, these defects are caused by noise—electrical interference in an image. It is usually caused when photos are shot at high ISO levels. In such cases, pixels become visible to the human eye. High noise levels often obscure details and can become a problem when photos are cropped and enlarged. When the noise-reduction option is used on photo-editing software, it eliminates odd pixels by changing them to match the colors of the surrounding area.

Removing noise causes an image to become less sharp, giving it an appearance of being out of focus or fuzzy. For this reason, some noise is desirable, as photographers Harold Davis and Phyllis Davis explain: "Noise can be a good thing. An image without noise can look 'toothless'—flat and lacking in texture. There are times where I either leave noise in a high noise image, or add noise on purpose."[15]

Combining Images

Noise reduction and color tinting are functions that are available on most photo-editing software. Advanced applications, such as Adobe Photoshop, allow users to create more-complex photos. For example, the advanced programs allow photographers to create composite images, or pictures made from several photos laid on top of one another. Because the photos are stacked, this function is called layers. Photography expert Tom Ang explains the use of layers: "You can place images on top of one another—varying the order in which they lie; duplicate smaller images and place them around the canvas to create a new image; or change the size of the individual components or distort them at will."[16]

Layers can be used in trick photography, which combines absurd elements, such as a giant mouse towering over the skyscrapers of Manhattan. Layers are also used when a photographer shoots several photos of the same scene using different aperture and ISO settings. For example, someone might take three photos of a mountain range with dramatic clouds floating above it and create one image. One of the photos might perfectly show the clouds, while the mountains below appear dark and shadowy. Another photo, shot with a different aperture setting, might show details of the mountain rocks and trees, while the clouds appear

In the photo-editing program Adobe Photoshop, layers can be used to create composite images combining multiple photos.

too bright. Perhaps a third shot was taken as an eagle flew through the sky, but the rest of the exposure was bad. Using layers, a photographer can layer all three of these exposures on top of one another. The result is a single stunning photo of mountains, clouds, rocks, trees, and an eagle.

Apps and Special Effects

Layering is complicated and requires skills on the part of the user. A photo editor might have to perform twenty or more separate steps with various controls in order to select, adjust, combine, and blend three photos. In the 2010s, much of this work has been taken over by apps.

Apple opened its App Store in 2008, a move that was quickly followed by Google Play. Both online stores feature

Video-Editing Apps

In an era where digital cameras can shoot video, the Internet is awash in applications that work with movies. Many free or inexpensive apps are simple to operate and perform like photography apps. Viddy allows users to add filters that enhance the look and feel of a video. Magisto lets users select themes and music. The software automatically selects the best scene from a video and creates short clips with no user input. Socialcam is the Instagram of videos. It allows users to add filters to their videos before uploading them to social networking sites, where viewers can add comments or choose to "Like" them. The Andromedia Video Editor can add transitions between scenes, insert still photos, and edit the audio. While video editing is one of the most complex processes a photographer can perform in a digital darkroom, inexpensive video apps make the work simple and easy.

a host of free or inexpensive apps used for trick photography and special effects. The most popular photo apps work with the built-in cameras found on smartphones and tablets. After a user snaps a photograph, apps can apply filters, borders, and special effects.

Instagram became an extremely popular photo app after it was released in 2010. Instagram is an easy-to-use app that offers nineteen effect filters. These can turn a photo black and white or give it the retro look of photos taken in past decades. Many filters are based on specific cameras and film used in the twentieth century. For example, several Instagram filters mimic the look of pictures taken with the Polaroid Land Camera. This camera was popular because it produced self-developing photographs that emerged from the camera after they were shot; it was not necessary to take Polaroid film in to be developed. Because of the chemical makeup of the Polaroid film, the photos had a somewhat washed-out appearance, which can be

The popular photo-editing and social networking app Instagram (shown on an iPhone around 2012) was released in 2010 and had more than 100 million users within two-and-half years.

obtained using the Instagram filter Brannan. Another Instagram filter, Hefe, mimics a type of Polaroid film called PZ 680. This film produced warm yellow and orange tones. The Instagram filter Walden imitates the cool, blue look of Polaroid PX 70 film.

It is easy to see why Instagram is so popular. While app users can create the Brannan effect with the touch of a finger, the same look requires a twenty-three-step process with Photoshop. These steps include creating layers and

Scanning Photos

Scanning is the process that converts film-based photographs into digital images that can be edited with photo software. A photo scanner operates much like a digital camera, using an image sensor, a bright light, mirrors, and a lens. These devices are attached to a mechanism called a scan head, which moves across the length of the scanner on a belt attached to a motor.

The scanning process begins when a photograph is laid on the flat glass plate of the scanner. A bright light on the scan head illuminates the photograph. The photo is reflected through a series of mirrors that focus the image onto a lens. This reflected light is converted into pixels by a CCD (charge-coupled device) image sensor. Most scanners use a three-pass system for each of the primary colors in the RGB system. Each pass places a different colored filter—red, green, or blue—in front of the CCD. Once this process is completed, the scanner software assembles the three filtered images into a full-color photograph made from pixels. This can be transferred to a computer through a USB cable or Wi-Fi connection.

changing brightness, contrast, tint, temperature, and color saturation levels. Imitating the Hefe filter requires sixteen steps with Photoshop.

Like many apps, Instagram has limits. Beyond selecting filters, there is little else users can do to manipulate photos. That has not affected Instagram's popularity. Initially released for Apple iPhones and iPads, the app was an instant hit. When Instagram created an app for the Android smartphone operating system in 2012, more than 1 million downloads were completed on the first day. That year, the company was purchased by Facebook for around $1 billion. By February 2013, the two-and-a-half-year-old service had more than 100 million users who were collectively uploading 40 million photos a day.

Cats and Cartoons

Instagram is among hundreds of apps designed to manipulate photos. Others provide even more narrowly defined functions. Vintage Scene makes photos look like they were taken in the nineteenth century. Color Splash lets users select parts of a photo to remain in color while other parts are transformed into black and white. There are apps to make people look old, apps to apply funny hairdos to subjects in portraits, and apps that make collages out of several photos.

ToonCamera allows users to give their photos a cartoon effect as if they were sketched by an artist. The Cats app replaces the heads of subjects with cat heads or adds cats to any scene that needs them. Rainy Daze makes subjects appear as if they were photographed standing in a dramatic rainstorm.

A laptop shows the photo-editing program Apple Aperture, a new competitor to Adobe Photoshop.

Organizing and Managing Photos

While most apps perform one or two functions well, advanced photo-editing software remains popular among shutterbugs who shoot hundreds or thousands of pictures a year. In addition to editing photos, advanced software offers numerous options to organize, view, print, and share photographs. Programs such as Lightroom and Aperture even offer users the option of creating professional-quality, hardcover photo books using online publishers.

For those who wish to print their own photos, editing programs provide multiple ways to display them. Users can drag photos from a toolbar into a large image window that offers print layout op-

tions. These include single shots, multiple images per page, or multipage photo essay.

While millions of people upload their photos to social networking sites, photo editors also offer the option for creating Web galleries. Once the photos are arranged to the user's satisfaction, the software uploads the Web page containing the images to the Internet.

A Range of Options

Adobe Photoshop is one of the most advanced programs for displaying, sharing, and altering images and was among the top-selling photo-editing programs in 2013. But it faced competition from at least fifty comparable applications, including Apple Aperture, GIMP, PhotoFiltre, and Artweaver. There also were dozens of free or inexpensive video-editing apps such as Socialcam, YouTube Capture, and Magisto.

It is not surprising that the number of photo editors has increased with digital camera ownership. Perhaps 10 percent of photographers had their own darkrooms in the film era; today anyone with a computer and basic apps possesses the ability to develop photos without a darkroom.

Photo manipulation has come a long way since the days of chemicals, enlargers, and safelights. Photographers have come out of the dark and into a pixelated world where fixing up a photograph is as easy as clicking a mouse.

CHAPTER 5

Photo Sharing, Privacy, and Other Concerns

E very photo-editor technology created since the mid-2000s offers multiple methods for sharing photos with friends, family, and strangers. One of the most popular software features uploads photographs directly to social media websites including Facebook, Twitter, and Flickr. Tens of millions of people use this tool every day, resulting in billions of photographs shared throughout the world. This was not always the case.

During the film era, photographs were physical objects that were stored in boxes or pasted into photo albums. Few people outside the photographer's immediate friends and family ever saw the pictures. Photos that were artistic or historic might be printed in books or displayed on the walls of galleries and museums. Newspaper and magazine photos were taken by professionals. There were few ways amateur photographers could share their pictures with the public at large, prompting tech writer Jonathan Margolis to note, "Photography used to be a bit elitist."[17]

Flickr's Photo Advances

The restrictions in photo sharing began to fall in the second half of the 1990s, when it became possible to attach digital photos to e-mails or publish them on websites. During this transitional era between film and digital cameras, most shared pictures originated as photographic prints digitized on a scanner. The first software dedicated to photo sharing, Kodak's EasyShare, was not marketed until 2001, the year before Nokia released the first cell phone camera. EasyShare provided a user-friendly, one-click system for transferring photos to a computer, sharing files by e-mail, and making prints. Around this time, several companies opened photo-sharing websites available to members. A site called Webshots had the largest online directory of photographs in the early 2000s. In 2012, it was renamed Smile, a service that offered users photo storage for an annual membership fee.

In 2004, the photo-sharing website Flickr appeared online and within a few months attracted more than 1 million users. The site was different from other photo-sharing websites and its unique design set the tone for those that followed. Social media expert Amy Rainey explains:

> [Flickr] allows people to comment on each other's photos, tag photos, post annotations and search through photos. Flickr allows for groups based on different themes and events. Flickr was immediately a hit with bloggers because of blog-friendly tools, like the ability to embed . . . photos in your blog or to automatically post camera phone shots to a blog.[18]

The Facebook Phenomenon

In March 2005, the Internet search engine Yahoo, recognizing the unique value of Flickr, purchased the photo-sharing site for $35 million. Six months later, Facebook, which was founded in February 2005, added a photo application. Like Flickr, Facebook allowed users to tag photos and make comments. By 2007, Facebook counted 20 million users, and that number rose sharply in the years that followed. By 2009, Facebook had 200 million users, and by 2013, more than 1.1 billion people were using the site.

As Facebook attracted new members, it became the largest photo-sharing website in the world. By 2013, Facebook held 240 billion individual photographs, and 2.1 billion new photos were uploaded to the site every week. That was equal

Founded in 2005, Facebook has grown to be the largest photo-sharing application in the world, holding more than 240 billion photographs in 2013.

to 109.5 billion photos per year—about 16 photos for every person on earth.

Facebook made photo sharing extremely easy with a tool called Photo Sync, which it introduced in late 2012. When the Photo Sync app was installed on a smartphone, it automatically uploaded all of the photographs taken with the digital camera. These photos were not posted to the user's Facebook page, but stored on a personal Photo Sync folder on the company's storage site. Photos were kept private unless users chose to post them on their Facebook page.

Privacy Concerns

Photo Sync was created to take advantage of the fact that 27 percent of all photographs in the United States in 2012 were taken with smartphones. While the service provided convenience for cell phone camera users, it also raised privacy concerns. Social media and photo-sharing websites such as Facebook make money from selling personal information about users to advertisers. Any information posted to these sites, including photographs, can be used to target consumers for ads. As computer security expert Graham Cluley explains:

> Photos taken on mobile devices can include [information] such as the location where the photo was

Manti Te'o's Online Impostor

In 2013, the problem of online impersonation made headlines when Notre Dame football star Manti Te'o revealed on Facebook that his girlfriend Lennay Kekua died of leukemia on September 11, 2012. Te'o gained the admiration of fans nationwide after it was reported he would not miss any games. Te'o told sports media outlets that he promised Kekua he would continue to play in her honor. There was one problem with Te'o's promise: Kekua did not exist.

Two reporters revealed that Kekua was a hoax, although Te'o himself did not know it. Kekua was invented by a man named Ronaiah Tuiasosopo, who was impersonating the fictitious woman to conduct an online relationship with Te'o. To create Kekua's identity, Tuiasosopo used a photograph of a twenty-three-year-old California woman named Diane O'Meara. Tuiasosopo later confessed to O'Meara that he had "stalked" her Facebook profile for five years and had stolen numerous photos she posted in order to create Kekua. O'Meara said she felt "violated" and "exposed" by what happened. However, Tuiasosopo did not break any laws, because he did not use his online impersonation to steal any money or financial information.

Quoted in Tami Abdollah. "Diane O'Meara, Woman in Manti Te'o Girlfriend Pictures, Says Ronaiah Tuiasosopo Confessed," *Huffington Post*, January 24, 2013. www.huffingtonpost.com/2013/01/24/diane-omeara-manti-teo-girlfriend-pictures_n_2546775.html.

taken—and this could be used to determine where you are, and help Facebook display localized advertising. Furthermore, Facebook could . . . analyze your photos [with facial recognition technology] to see whose faces it recognizes and automatically tag their names. Over time a comprehensive database of where you have been, and who with, is built up.[19]

HOW DOES FACIAL RECOGNITION TECHNOLOGY WORK?

Facial recognition systems are trained to recognize known faces using specific facial features of known persons. Different modules in the system determine how similar or dissimilar specific regions of the face are to each face stored in the database.

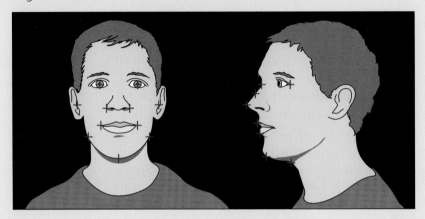

Facial recognition systems receive video streams from surveillance cameras. First they determine which parts of the image are faces. The images of the faces are then analyzed and compared with the data stored in the database to determine identity.

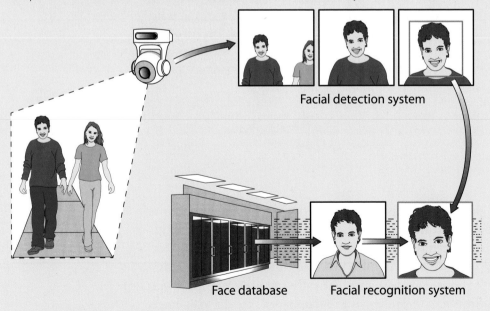

Facial detection system

Face database   Facial recognition system

Facial recognition technology uses features such as the shape of the eyes, nose, and cheekbones to match images. While this technology is popular among advertisers, it is also being used by police departments and government investigators. For example, in 2013, the New York City Police Department set up a Facial Recognition Unit to scan faces on Instagram and Facebook. The unit used surveillance-camera footage from crime scenes and matched them to mug shots (arrest photos) of known criminals. When matched to faces on social media sites, police were able to discover addresses, phone numbers, and other information about suspects.

Photo Sharing and Criminals

Sometimes criminals make it easy for police by bragging about their illegal activities on Facebook. Some even include incriminating photographs. This was the case of two men in Utah who set up potentially deadly booby traps on a popular hiking trail in April 2012. The devices were medieval; they were large rocks with sharp, pointy sticks tied to them. When set off by a trip wire, the devices were made to swing down on a rope and hit victims in the face. The men were caught after chatting about the traps on Facebook and posting a picture of the deadly device. Winston Ross, a national correspondent for *The Daily Beast*, explains why people incriminate themselves on Facebook: "[They possess a] self-destructive combination of ignorance, narcissism, and generation-specific disregard for their own privacy. . . . [S]ome users were willing to do just about anything for attention. If status updates didn't get a rise out of followers, they'd post pictures."[20]

Most people do not post incriminating pictures online, but there are also dangers associated with innocently posting personal photographs on photo-sharing websites. According to a 2012 study by Carnegie Mellon University (CMU), Facebook photos could theoretically be used by criminals searching for sensitive information.

In one experiment, CMU researchers used a widely available facial recognition app to identify individuals on a popular online dating site. Although users of the dating site protect their privacy through pseudonyms (made-up names), the technology was used to link faces to photos on Facebook. Researchers used other publicly available data to discover the sexual orientation, credit scores, and other personal information about subjects.

In a second experiment, researchers took snapshots of anonymous volunteers with a webcam set up in the student union. They were able to identify about one-third of the students in less than one minute using facial recognition software and Facebook photos. The identities were matched with birthdays and hometowns of the

Facial recognition equipment is demonstrated at a 2002 security technology show in Germany to identify persons using surveillance camera footage.

subjects. Using a computer algorithm developed by CMU, the information was used to accurately predict the Social Security numbers of volunteers. Criminals often use this information to commit identity theft—stealing someone's personal information to apply for credit cards and bank loans. Carnegie Mellon professor Alessandro Acquisti, who headed the project, commented:

> I wanted to see if it was possible to go from a face on the street to a Social Security Number. . . . There's a blending of online and offline data, and your face is the conduit—the veritable link between these two worlds. I think the lesson is a rather gloomy one. We have to face the reality that our very notion of privacy is being eroded. You're no longer private in the street or in a crowd."[21]

Although CMU researchers did not reveal their exact methods, there is little doubt that tech-savvy criminals are

The Video Voyeurism Prevention Act

As the popularity of cell phone cameras exploded in the mid-2000s, there were a growing number of places where the devices were not welcome. Schools banned camera phones because they could be used to cheat on tests. Courthouses banned them to protect the identity of undercover police officers. Major corporations such as General Motors, Intel, and Lockheed Martin prohibited the use of the cameras in some areas because they might be used to steal company secrets. In addition, small digital cameras increasingly were used to spy on people in department store dressing rooms, locker rooms, and tanning salons. These photos were sometimes posted to pornographic websites without the victims' knowledge.

In 2004 the U.S. Congress reacted to this problem and passed the Video Voyeurism Prevention Act. The law prohibits the covert photographing or videotaping of a naked person in a gym, tanning salon, dressing room, or anywhere else where one expects a "reasonable expectation of privacy." Violators can be fined up to $100,000 and receive up to a year in prison.

working to conduct similar searches. It is conceivable that someone could eventually invent an app to steal identities with the click of a mouse.

Posting Without Permission

There are laws against stealing a person's financial information. However, in most states it is not illegal to steal a person's online identity as long as no money is taken. Online identity theft happens when a perpetrator pretends to be someone else. They use a victim's photograph, name, and profile information to set up pages on social media websites.

The impersonator might use the false identity to ruin a victim's reputation or lure someone into a sexual relationship.

One example of online identity theft was traced to a sixteen-year-old girl in Toronto, Canada. In 2012, she set up a Facebook account using the name and downloaded photographs of a teenage boy she wished to harass. For eleven months, the suspect used the fake account to send insulting remarks to the victim's friends and others. These remarks compromised the victim's relationships with people at school and caused him great distress before the scheme was uncovered.

The YouTube Effect

While photo sharing has changed personal social interactions, it has also transformed the way people see the world. In the twentieth century, when important news unfolded, people turned on their televisions and radios to find out the details. In the twenty-first century, the most up-to-date news can often be found on the Internet, with social media websites leading the way. This phenomenon can be traced to September 2004, when terrorists in Jakarta, Indonesia, set off a car bomb in front of the Australian embassy, killing 11 and wounding 150. The first pictures of the incident did not come from professional photojournalists, but from bystanders who posted cell phone photographs of the incident on Flickr. Several months later, a deadly tsunami swept through the Thailand resort town of Khao Lak after an earthquake, killing more than 4,000 people. The only pictures available for twenty-four hours after the incident were those posted by survivors who recorded the event with their digital cameras.

Amateur news reporting took another step forward after YouTube was launched in November 2005. While most of the sixty-five thousand new videos uploaded to the site every day in 2006 were parties, pets, sports, and vacation videos, the site also contained videos shot by terrorists, political activists, and American soldiers fighting in Iraq. Some of this footage was redistributed by bloggers, uploaded to social media websites, and even rebroadcast by mainstream television news networks.

YouTube not only changed the way videos were shared, it also added new words to the English language. Clips that were watched, shared, and rebroadcast thousands of times were said to be viral videos. The term "YouTube effect" was used to describe the phenomenon of people uploading videos from political events that were otherwise ignored by the mainstream media. Moisés Naím, editor in chief of *Foreign Policy*, explains the YouTube effect:

> Activists everywhere are recognizing the power of citizen-produced and Web-distributed videos as the ultimate testimony. The human rights group Witness arms individuals in conflict zones with video cameras so they can record and expose human rights abuses. Electoral watchdogs are taping elections. Even Islamic terrorists have adapted to this trend. [The terrorist organization] Al Qaeda created a special media production unit called Al Sahab ("The Cloud"), which routinely posts its videos online, with the realistic expectation that they will be picked up by major media outlets and other Web sites.[22]

A screen grab from a video uploaded to YouTube shows anti-government demonstrators marching in Latakia, Syria, on August 12, 2011.

Naím described the YouTube effect in late 2006, a breakthrough year for viral videos. One of the most talked about was the execution of deposed Iraqi dictator Saddam Hussein, who had been convicted of crimes against the people of Iraq. When Hussein was hanged, an attending soldier shot video footage of the execution with his cell phone camera. The video, complete with the dictator marching up the steps of the gallows while being taunted by his executioners, immediately went viral and was shown repeatedly on television news shows throughout the world.

The YouTube effect was credited with driving the events known as the Arab Spring. Beginning in December 2010, a revolutionary wave of massive political demonstrations swept through Tunisia, Egypt, Libya, Yemen, and other Middle Eastern countries. Protesters were met with swift and violent retaliation from police and soldiers. While government officials censored news reports about the demonstrations, cell phone cameras wielded by young, media-savvy protestors captured tanks rolling through the streets, police battling protesters, and even people being killed in melees.

The high-quality cell phone videos and photographs of the Arab Spring were picked up by major media outlets, including CNN and the *New York Times*. As Turi Munthe, the founder of the citizen journalism service Demotix, said at the time:

> Broadcasters are going out of their way to use cameraphones because the images look more authentic. In almost every image of Tahrir Square [site of protests in Cairo, Egypt] there were people waving cameraphones. . . . We had close to 1,000 contributors shipping us images from North Africa. In Egypt, there was a feeling the war was being waged on two fronts—the war against [Egyptian dictator Hosni] Mubarak and the campaign to get the uprising all over the media.[23]

Protesters succeeded in showing the world the harsh, repressive conditions that governed their lives. To battle the YouTube effect, government officials blocked public access to Facebook, YouTube, and other social media sites. In addition, police scoured the images to identify protest leaders, many of whom were arrested.

Digital Video Surveillance

In addition to the digital images on Facebook and YouTube, authorities had their own images of the Arab Spring protests. These came from tiny surveillance video cameras, which can be found in cities throughout the world.

In past decades, closed-circuit television (CCTV) cameras were large and expensive. The grainy videos they created were of poor quality. In recent years, digital surveillance cameras have decreased in cost and size, while picture quality has drastically improved. High-quality CCTV systems are available at electronics stores, and the cameras can be monitored on a smart phone, laptop, or tablet computer. Little wonder the number of surveillance cameras rapidly grew in the 2010s, with large cities leading the way.

In 2013, New York City had more than four thousand cameras watching over citizens in Manhattan. Thousands more were deployed in the city's boroughs, including the Bronx, Brooklyn, and Queens. The cameras, which were difficult to see with an untrained eye, were located on building facades, storefronts, and light poles. Between 2001 and 2013, Chicago installed an estimated ten thousand public and private security cameras, many of them inside passenger train cars on the city's rail system. As former Homeland Security secretary Michael Chertoff stated, "I don't think there is another city in the U.S. that has as an extensive and integrated camera network as Chicago has."[24]

Monitoring Everyone

While thousands of cameras operate in Chicago and New York, London, England, has often been called the most surveilled city in the world. After suicide bombers killed fifty-two people on London's public transportation systems in July 2005, the city installed more than a half-million surveillance cameras at a cost of more than $750 million.

A CCTV
surveillance camera
keeps watch over the
public area outside
the King's Cross rail
station in London,
England, in this
photo from 2013.

Critics of widespread government surveillance often point out that video cameras do not prevent crime. The crime rates in London, Chicago, and New York are not significantly lower than comparable cities without massive surveillance. In addition, the cameras do not help solve crimes once they are committed. A 2008 study by London's Metropolitan Police Department showed that only one crime was solved for every one thousand cameras in the city. While questioning the value of surveillance cameras, critics note that they represent government intrusion into private lives. As Matthew Elliot, of the British anti-surveillance organization Big Brother Watch, states, governments "continue to pour huge amounts of money into technology that indiscriminately monitors us all as potential criminals, while the actual causes of crime go ignored. Britain has become one of the most 'watched' societies in the world, far outstripping some authoritarian regimes."[25]

Boston Marathon Bombings

Whatever the criticism, surveillance cameras proved to be useful during an April 2013 terrorist attack during which two bombs exploded near the finish line of the Boston Marathon. The incident, planned by two brothers, Dzhokhar and Tamerlan Tsarnaev, killed 3 and injured 264.

Many people were already photographing and videotaping the marathon when the bombs went off; others pulled out their cell phone cameras seconds after the two explosions, which were about one block apart. Within minutes, hundreds of images were circulating on photo-sharing and social media websites. While some photos showed the general carnage and confusion at the scene, others were thought to show evidence of the crime. As forensic video analyst Grant Fredericks stated, "[The] general public is collecting video evidence every moment of every day."[26] In an unprecedented move, the Federal Bureau of Investigation (FBI) asked citizens to help find the bombers by submitting digital images from the event. Authorities were quickly overwhelmed by the thousands of photos and videos captured by citizens; however, none of the materials proved to be useful.

The Boston Marathon bombing suspects were eventually identified by video surveillance cameras located outside a department store near one of the bomb blasts. The role played by social media became a story in itself, as it exposed many of the problems associated with photo-sharing websites. In the rush to capture the suspect, photographs of bystanders carrying large bags near the bomb blasts were hastily posted on Facebook, Flickr, Twitter, and other sites. The social networking site Reddit received thousands of posts containing inappropriate and incorrect material. Innocent people were accused of terrorism and threatened with bodily harm. Personal information about these people, including phone numbers, addresses, and Facebook homepage links, was posted online.

Reporters were among the people searching Reddit for breaking news. The front page of the *New York Post* even featured a photograph of two innocent high school students carrying backpacks under the headline "Bag Men." While

Mistaken Identity in Boston Bombing

The Boston Marathon bomb attack on April 15, 2013, shined a light on privacy issues associated with photo sharing and social media. The social networking site Reddit was at the center of an uproar after one of its users set up a forum called FindBostonBombers immediately after the bombing. Visitors to the site were asked to examine the massive number of photos of the bomb site that had surfaced on Facebook, Flickr, Twitter, and other sites.

On April 19, 2013, a young woman on Twitter identified a twenty-two-year-old Brown University student named Sunil Triphathi as one of the bombing suspects. Triphathi had been reported missing by his family on March 16. The woman's tweet was posted on FindBostonBombers, which had nine thousand followers by this time. The mainstream news agency Reuters soon announced that Triphathi was a suspect in the bombing. Triphathi's family received death threats, while strangers posted angry comments on the missing man's Facebook page. On April 25, Triphathi was found dead in the ocean near Providence, Rhode Island. Authorities said he had been in the water for some time. When the news of his death was reported, the same sites that accused Triphathi of being a terrorist were filled with outpourings of grief.

they received no apology, the students were quickly exonerated on other media sites.

As the Boston photo-sharing frenzy proved, the border between public places and private lives was being erased. However, polls show that most citizens do not mind being watched by digital surveillance cameras while out in public. A 2013 *New York Times* poll showed that 78 percent of Americans agreed with the statement "surveillance cameras [are] a good idea."[27]

Cameras on Eyeglasses

While surveillance cameras might record people walking down the street, the images generally are not available for viewing to just anyone with an Internet connection. However, the same cannot be said for Google Street View, the mapping service that provides panoramic photographs of millions of streets throughout the world.

After Google Street View was launched in 2007, the company used camera-equipped cars to photograph nearly every building and every street in the United States. In the following years, Street View grew to include portions of forty-eight other countries. Street View images can be seen by users of Google Maps and Google Earth.

Street View has been helpful to countless people looking for unfamiliar addresses, but privacy advocates have objected to this popular feature. They point out that the cameras have captured private actions most would not wish to have been published online. Controversial images include sunbathers in bikinis and people leaving strip clubs and abortion clinics. While Google blurs faces of people caught on Street View cameras, many can be identified by their clothing or profile.

In 2013, Google pushed privacy boundaries even further with the introduction of Google Glass, a mini computer

A woman tests Google Glass at a technology conference in May 2013 in San Francisco, California.

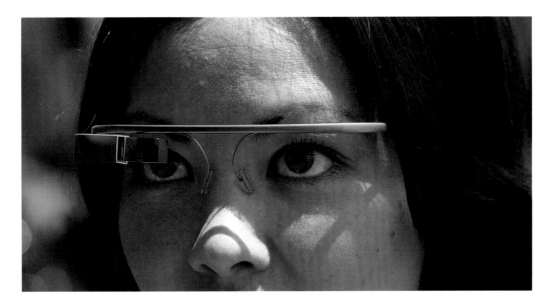

worn like a pair of glasses. Google Glass takes photos and records high-definition videos with a simple voice command. These can be instantly uploaded to the Internet. In addition, there was an app that allowed users to snap pictures simply by winking.

Google Glass raised a host of privacy issues. The built-in camera could be used to invade privacy and record people without their permission. As a result, wearers of Google Glass were banned in some bars in Seattle and in Las Vegas casinos, where there were fears the devices might be used to cheat at card games or record concerts. Concerns were also raised when a programmer named Liam McLoughlin was able to hack into Glass. This allowed him to take control of the device worn by another person. Computer security expert Jay Freeman describes why he was alarmed by McLoughlin's actions:

> Once the attacker has root on your Glass, they have much more power than if they had access to your phone or even your computer: they have control over a camera and a microphone that are attached to your head. A bugged Glass doesn't just watch your every move: it watches everything you are looking at (intentionally or furtively) and hears everything you do. The only thing it doesn't know are your thoughts.[28]

While digital cameras large and small have reshaped the world, they also have posed unanswered questions and created new problems. When people were clicking away on Polaroids and SLRs in the 1970s, the idea of an eyeglass camera that could instantly broadcast photos and videos to the entire world was the stuff of science fiction. The large cameras of the era could not be smuggled into locker rooms, used for identity theft, or put to work by spies. Nor could they be used to click thousands of pictures for free to be shared with friends, family, and strangers. Whatever the drawbacks of a surveilled society, digital cameras are just one more way people can share their joys, pains, and pleasures with one another. In this way, the widespread availability of cheap, portable digital cameras has changed society and remade the world.

Chapter 1: Dissecting a Digital Camera

1. Ansel Adams. *The Camera*. Boston: Little, Brown & Company, 1989, p. 43.
2. Marc Spiwak. "Camcorders: A General Overview." B&H Photo and Electronics, May 2, 2011. www .bhphotovideo.com/indepth/video /buying-guides/camcorders-gen eral-overview.
3. David D. Busch, *Digital SLR Photography*. Boston: Course Technology, 2012, p. 14.

Chapter 2: Camera Modes and Settings

4. David Raboin. "What Is ISO and a Deeper Look at Your Image Sensor." Photos4U2C, January 9, 2011. www.photos4u2c.net/2010/11/27 /what-is-iso-and-a-deeper-look-at -your-image-sensor.
5. Natalie Norton. "4 Reasons Not to Write Off Shooting in Automatic." DPS, 2012. http://digital-photogra phy-school.com/4-reasons-not-to -write-off-shooting-in-automatic.
6. Ibarionex Perello. "Focus: The Eyes Have It." Peachpit, July 23, 2012.

www.peachpit.com/articles/article .aspx?p=1926196&seqNum=8.
7. Fred Hanselmann. "To Use a Tripod or Not?" Rocky Mountain Photography, March 2008. www .hanselmannphotography.com/All Articles/Tripods.html.

Chapter 3: Camcorders vs. Still Cameras

8. Steve Sanders. "How to Use Image Stabilization on a Camcorder." Steve's Digicams, 2013. www.steves -digicams.com/knowledge-center /how-tos/camcorder-operation/ how-to-use-image-stabilization -on-a-camcorder.html#b.
9. Josh Lehrer. "What to Look for in a HD Digital Camcorder." Adorama, October 24, 2012. www.adorama .com/alc/0012078/article/How-to -choose-a-camcorder.
10. Steve Sanders. "Understanding Video Camcorder Face Detection." Steve's Digicams, 2013. www.steves -digicams.com/knowledge-center /how-tos/camcorder-operation /understanding-video-camcorder -face-detection.html#b.
11. Quoted in Sam Grobart and Evelyn M. Rusli. "For Flip Video

Camera, Four Years from Hot Start-up to Obsolete." *New York Times*, April 12, 2011. www.nytimes.com/2011/04/13/technology/13flip.html?_r=0.

12. Tim Peterson. "GoPro Boosts Sales via Snap and Share." *AdWeek*, January 29, 2013. www.adweek.com/news/technology/gopro-boosts-sales-snap-and-share-146821.

Chapter 4: The Digital Darkroom

13. Ansel Adams. *The Print*. Boston: Little, Brown & Company, 2003, p. 1.

14. Amadou Diallo. "Printer Primer 1: Choosing a Photo Printer." DPReview, January 28, 2013. www.dpreview.com/articles/1690328781/printer-primer-1-choosing-a-photo-printer.

15. Harold Davis and Phyllis Davis. *The Photoshop Darkroom*. Burlington, MA: Focal Press, 2010, p. 70.

16. Tom Ang. *Digital Photographer's Handbook*. New York: DK Publishing, 2012, p. 278.

Chapter 5: Photo Sharing, Privacy, and Other Concerns

17. Quoted in Tom de Castella. "Five Ways the Digital Camera Changed Us." BBC News, January 12, 2012. www.bbc.co.uk/news/mobile/magazine-16483509.

18. Amy Rainey. "Evolution of Digital Photo Sharing Services." August 5, 2010. http://amyrainey.wordpress.com/2010/08/05/evolution-of-digital-photo-sharing-services.

19. Graham Cluley. "Facebook Photo Sync: Nine Things You Should Know." Naked Security, December 3, 2012. http://nakedsecurity.sophos.com/2012/12/03/facebook-photo-sync-things-should-know.

20. Winston Ross. "Fugitives Who Love Facebook: The Next Big Crime Wave." *The Daily Beast*, April 15, 2012. www.thedailybeast.com/articles/2012/04/15/fugitives-who-love-facebook-the-next-big-crime-wave.html.

21. Quoted in Paul Roberts. "How Facebook and Facial Recognition Are Creating a Minority Report-Style Privacy Meltdown." Threat Post, August 5, 2011. http://threatpost.com/how-facebook-and-facial-recognition-are-creating-minority-report-style-privacy-meltdown-080511.

22. Moisés Naím. "The YouTube Effect." *Foreign Policy*, December 27, 2006. www.foreignpolicy.com/articles/2006/12/27/the_youtube_effect.

23. Quoted in David Batty. "Arab Spring Leads Surge in Events Captured on Cameraphones." *Guardian*, December 29, 2011. www.guardian.co.uk/world/2011/dec/29/arab-spring-captured-on-cameraphones.

24. Quoted in "Welcome to Chicago, Most Surveilled City in the World." NBC Chicago, April 6, 2010. www

.nbcchicago.com/news/local/Welcome-to-Chicago-Most-Surveilled-City-in-the-World-89991502.html #ixzz2TIq1bi6X.

25. Matthew Elliot. "The Price of Privacy: Councils Spend Half a Billion Pounds on CCTV in Four Years." Big Brother Watch, 2013. www.bigbrotherwatch.org.uk/home/2012/02/price-privacy-councils-spend-521m.html.

26. Quoted in Matt Stroud. "In Boston Bombing, Flood of Digital Evidence Is a Blessing and a Curse." *The Verge*, April 16, 2013. www.theverge.com/2013/4/16/4230820/in-boston-bombing-flood-of-digital-evidence-is-a-blessing-and-a-curse.

27. Quoted in Eyder Peralta. "Poll: Most Americans Are OK with Surveillance Cameras." NPR, April 30, 2013. www.npr.org/blogs/thetwo-way/2013/04/30/180159756/poll-most-americans-are-ok-with-surveillance-cameras.

28. Quoted in Beck Alleman. "As Google Glass Nears Release, Legal Problems Arise." IVN, May 6, 2013. http://ivn.us/2013/05/06/as-google-glass-nears-release-legal-problems-arise.

GLOSSARY

aperture: A series of overlapping plates in a lens that can be dialed open to let in more light or closed to let in less light.

cityscape: The urban version of a landscape, in which a portion of a city is used as a subject in a photograph or painting.

crop: To frame an image by selecting a portion of it and removing outer parts.

demosaicing: A process that reconstructs a full-color image from the output of a digital camera image sensor.

depth of field: The distance between the nearest and farthest objects in a scene that appear to be in sharp focus.

focal point: The point at which an image is created after light passes through a lens.

geotagging: The process of using GPS technology to add geographical data such as longitude and latitude to a photograph so the exact location is recorded.

globally: In photo editing, it refers to the entire area of a photograph overall, not a specific, smaller area of a photo.

panning: Turning a camera from side to side to keep the subject in the viewfinder.

photon: An elementary particle, or bundle, of light energy.

portrait: A picture of a person, usually the face and upper body.

FOR MORE INFORMATION

Books

Roman Espejo, ed. *Smartphones*. Farmington Hills, MI: Greenhaven, 2013. This title from the Opposing Viewpoints series examines the controversies presented by the growing number of smartphones in the world, including issues of privacy.

Thom Gaines. *Digital Photo Madness!: 50 Weird and Wacky Things to Do with Your Digital Camera*. Asheville, NC: Lark, 2010. The book explains everything from using the camera to coordinating it with the computer, printer, and scanner.

Ashley Rae Harris. *Facebook: The Company and Its Founders*. Minneapolis: Abdo, 2012. This title examines the lives of Mark Zuckerberg, Eduardo Saverin, Dustin Moskovitz, and Chris Hughes and their work building the social networking site Facebook.

Harry Henderson. *The Digital Age*. San Diego: ReferencePointPress, 2012. This title is a thorough examination of the role computers have played in world history in the past half-century, including the development of online music and video resources and the explosion of social networking in recent years.

Troy Lanier and Clay Nichols. *Filmmaking for Teens: Pulling Off Your Shorts*. Studio City, CA: Michael Wiese Productions, 2010. Written by two teachers of filmmaking in Austin, Texas, this book explains how to make a short film by writing a script and working as a producer, director, and editor.

Carla Killough McClafferty. *Profiles #3: Tech Titans*. New York: Scholastic, 2012. This book explores the lives of the people who have had a huge impact on technology today, including Bill Gates, Steve Jobs, Mark Zuckerberg, Larry Page, and Sergey Brin.

Brenda Tharp and Jed Manwaring. *Extraordinary Everyday Photography: Awaken Your Vision to Create Stunning Images Wherever You Are*. New York: Amphoto, 2012. An easy-to-use guide about capturing light, landscapes, wildlife, and people, with examples from the authors, taken with DSLRs, compact digital cameras, and iPhones.

Websites

Exposure Guide (www.exposureguide .com). This website displays photographs shot by professionals and features camera basics, photography tips and techniques, image-editing advice, and blogs.

Flickr (www.flickr.com). This photo- and video-sharing site, founded in 2004, set the tone for the social media sites that followed. Having uploaded more than 6 billion images, Flickr's 51 million members can post, comment, and share images.

Metacafe (www.metacafe.com). This video-sharing site pays people for posting short, original videos. If a video is popular among users and hits twenty thousand views, Metacafe pays $5 for every one thousand views.

Reddit (www.reddit.com). This social news and entertainment site allows users to submit self-generated content such as photos and videos, or links to other sites. Users vote on submissions, which are moved up or down on page listings.

YouTube (www.youtube.com). People watch 6 billion hours of video each month on this video-sharing website. From cute pet movies to bloody war videos, this site has changed the way people view the world.

INDEX

A

Adobe Lightroom (software), 68
Adobe Photoshop (software), 63, *64*, 69, 75
Analog-to-digital converters (ADC), 23, 47
Aperture
  in camcorders, 54
  manual adjustments, 42
  overview, 18–20, *19*
  working with, 40
Aperture (software), 63, *74*
Apple App Store, 70–71
Apps and special effects, 70–73
Arab Spring, 86
Artweaver (software), 75
Auditory feedback, 26
Auto mode, 35–36, *36*
Autofocus (AF) systems, 30–31, 33, 54
Automatic enhance controls, 64–65

B

Blemish fixes, 65
Boston Marathon bombings, 89–90
Brightness controls, 66

C

Camcorders
  face detection mode, 54
  flash cards, 52
  helmet cams, *55*, 56
  high definition, 50
  mics and sound, 52–53, *53*

miniDV cassettes, 51, *51*
modes, 53–54
overview, 46, *47*
similarities, 46–47
sports, *55*, 55–56
3-D, 57–59
wireless, 54–55
zooms, 47–50
Canon 7D DSLR, 49
Carnegie Mellon University (CMU), 81–82
Cell phone cameras. *See* Smartphones
Charge-coupled device (CCD), 22, 24, 73
Cisco Systems, 50
Closed-circuit television (CCTV), 87
Color temperature and tint, *67*, 67–68
Combining images, 69–70, *70*
Complementary metaloxide semiconductor (CMOS), 22
Contrast controls, 66
Cropping, 65–66

D

DCS-100 camera, 24
Demosaicing, defined, 23–24
Depth of field, *31*, 31–33
Digital cameras
  aperture, 18–20, *19*, *30*, 31–33
  flash feature, 25–26
  functions and features, 26–28
  image sensor, 22
  introduction of, *11*, 11–12

Q

Quartz timer, 26

R

Rainy Daze (app), 74
Read-only memory (ROM), 29
Red-eye fixes, 65
Reddit, 89–90
RGB color system, 63–64

S

Samsung digital camera, *14*
Sasson, Steven, 24
Scanners/scanning folders, 62, 73
Secure digital (SD) format, 25
Shotgun microphones, 53, *53*
Shutter/shutter speed, 20, 33, 43, *44*, 54
Sigma lens, 18
Smartphones
    apps for, 43, 70–73
    cameras in, 20
    modes, 29
    passive autofocus, 30
    special effects, 70–73
    3-D technology, 59
Sports camcorders, *55*, 55–56
Sports mode, 38–39, *39*
Stand-alone digital cameras, 20–21, 29
Standard-definition (SD) camcorder, 50
Straightening digital photos, 65–66

T

Telephoto lenses, 15
Te'o, Manti, 79
3-D camcorders, 57–59
Through-the-lens (TTL) viewing, 21, 27
ToonCamera (app), 74
Triphathi, Sunil, 90

Tuiasosopo, Ronaiah, 79
Twitter, 90

U

Ultra-optical zooms, 47
Ultra-wide-angle lenses, 16
Ultraviolet (UV) filters, 68

V

Variator group of lens, 18
Video sharing, 12
Video surveillance, 87
Video Voyeurism Prevention Act (2004),
   83
Video-editing apps, 71
Viewfinder, 20–22, *21*
Vintage Scene (app), 74
Viral videos, 85

W

Water mode, 44, *44*
Webshots, 77
Wi-Fi, in digital cameras, 26–28
Wide-angle lenses, 15
Wireless camcorders, 54–55
Woodman, Nick, 56

X

Xenon gas atoms, 26
XLR adapters, 53

Y

YouTube, 84–87, *85*

Z

Zoom lenses, 16, 17, 26, 47–50

PICTURE CREDITS

Cover: © artromashka/Shutterstock
  .com
© AFP Photo/YouTube/Getty Images,
  85
© Buzz Pictures/Alamy, 47
© Caro/Alamy, 82
© Chris Rutter/Digital Camera Maga-
  zine via Getty Images, 44
© Damian Turski/Getty Images, 41
© Dani Pozo/AFP/Getty Images,
  39
© Daniel Sousa/Alamy, 9
© David Caudery/Digital Camera
  Magazine via Getty Images, 21
© David Cayless/Getty Images, 38
© Dimitri Otis/Getty Images, 19
© Gale, Cengage Learning, 17, 32, 58,
  67, 80
© Ijansempoi/Shutterstock.com, 9
© Joby Sessions/Photo Plus Magazine
  via Getty Images, 36

© Jonathan Larsen/Diadem Images/
  Alamy, 53
© Justin Sullivan/Getty Images, 72, 78,
  91
© Leo/Shutterstock.com, 51
© Leon Neal/AFP/Getty Images, 88
© Mark Phillips/Alamy, 64
© Michael Marquand/Getty Images,
  31
© Mladen Antonov/AFP/Getty Im-
  ages, 55
© Nico Traut/Shutterstock.com, 16
© Peter Dazeley/Getty Images, 23
© Philip Sowels/MacFormat magazine
  via Getty Images, 74
© Realimage/Alamy, 61
© Science & Society Picture Library/
  Getty Images, 8, 11
© Sean Gallup/Getty Images, 14
© Studio 101/Alamy, 70
© Tim Ridley/Getty Images, 8

ABOUT THE AUTHOR

Stuart A. Kallen is the author of more than 250 nonfiction books for children and young adults. He has written extensively about science, the environment, music, history, and folklore (from vampires to haunted houses). In addition, Kallen has written award-winning children's videos and television scripts. In his spare time, he sings, writes songs, and plays the guitar. Kallen lives in San Diego, California.